Central Themes and Principles of Ericksonian Therapy

Ericksonian Monographs

Central Themes and Principles of Ericksonian Therapy

Edited by Stephen R. Lankton

Brunner/Mazel Publishers • New York

Library of Congress Cataloging-in-Publication Data

Central themes and principles of
  Ericksonian Therapy
    (Ericksonian monographs; no. 2)
    Includes bibliographies.
    1. Erickson, Milton H.   2. Psychotherapy.
3. Hypnotism—Therapeutic use.   I. Lankton, Stephen R.
II. Erickson, Milton H.   III. Series.   [DNLM: 1. Family
Therapy.   2. Hypnosis.   W1 ER44 no. 2 / WM 415 C397]
RC495.C45   1987   616.89′156   87-13831
ISBN 0-87630-470-6

Copyright © 1987 by The Milton H. Erickson Foundation

Published by
BRUNNER/MAZEL, INC.
19 Union Square
New York, New York 10003

MANUFACTURED IN THE UNITED STATES OF AMERICA

10   9   8   7   6   5   4   3   2   1

Ericksonian Monographs

Ericksonian Monographs publishes only original manuscripts dealing with Ericksonian approaches to hypnosis, family therapy, and psychotherapy, including techniques, case studies, research and theory.

The *Monographs* will publish only those articles of highest quality that foster the growth and development of the Ericksonian approach and exemplify an original contribution to the fields of physical and mental health. In keeping with the purpose of the *Monographs*, articles should be prepared so that they are readable to a heterogeneous audience of professionals in psychology, medicine, social work, dentistry and related clinical fields.

Abstracts of each article are on file at the Milton H. Erickson Foundation, Inc., in the following languages: French, German, Italian, and Spanish.

Publication of the *Ericksonian Monographs* shall be on an irregular basis; no more than three times per year. The *Monographs* are a numbered, periodical publication. Dates of publication are determined by the quantity of high quality articles accepted by the Editorial Board and the Board of Directors of the Milton H. Erickson Foundation, Inc., rather than calendar dates.

Manuscripts should be *submitted in quintuplicate* (5 copies) with a 100–150-word abstract to Stephen R. Lankton, M.S.W., P.O. Box 958, Gulf Breeze, Florida 32561-0958. Manuscripts of length ranging from 15 to 100 typed double-spaced pages will be considered for publication. Submitted manuscripts cannot be returned to authors. Authors with telecommunication capability may presubmit one copy electronically in either 1200 or 300 baud rate and the following communication parameters: 8 bit word size, No parity, 1 stop bit, x-on/x-off enabled, ASCII and xmodem transfer protocols are acceptable. Call (904) 932-6819 to arrange transmission and security passwords.

Style and format of submitted manuscripts must adhere to instructions described in the *Publication Manual of the American Psychological Associa-*

v

76444

tion (3rd edition, 1983). The manuscripts will be returned for revision if reference citations, preparation of tables and figures, manuscript format, avoidance of sexist language, copyright permission for cited material, title page style, etc. do not conform to the *Manual.*

Copyright ownership must be transferred to the Milton H. Erickson Foundation, Inc., if your manuscript is accepted for publication. The Editor's acceptance letter will include a form explaining copyright release, ownership and privileges.

Reference citations should be scrutinized with special care to credit originality and avoid plagiarism. Referenced material should be carefully checked by the author prior to first submission of the manuscript.

Charts and photographs accompanying the manuscripts must be presented in camera-ready form.

Copy editing and galley proofs will be sent to the authors for revisions. Manuscripts must be submitted in clearly written, acceptable, scholarly English. Neither the Editor nor the Publisher is responsible for correcting errors of spelling and grammar: the manuscript, after acceptance, should be immediately ready for publication. Authors should understand there will be a charge passed on to them by the Publisher for revision of galleys.

Prescreening and review procedures for articles is outlined below. Priority is given to those articles which conform to the designated theme for the upcoming *Monographs.* All manuscripts will be prescreened, absented of the author's name, by the Editor or one member of the Editorial Board and one member of either the Continuing Medical Education Committee or the Board of Directors of the Milton H. Erickson Foundation, Inc.

Final acceptance of all articles is done at the discretion of the Board of Directors of the Milton H. Erickson Foundation, Inc. Their decisions will be made after acceptable prescreened articles have been reviewed and edited by a minimum of four persons: two Editorial Board members, one member of the CME Committee or the Board of Directors, and the Editor. Occasionally, reviewers selected by the Editor will assist in compiling feedback to authors.

Feedback for authors and manuscript revision will be handled by the Editor usually between one and two months after submission of the prepared manuscript. Additional inquiries are welcomed if addressed to the Editor.

Contents

BOOK REVIEWS

Contributors

James R. Allen, M.D.
Professor, Department of Psychiatry and Behavioral Sciences, University of Oklahoma Tulsa Medical College, Tulsa, Oklahoma; Chief of Staff, Children's Medical Center, Tulsa, Oklahoma

Eric R. Aronson, Psy.D. Cand.
Doctoral candidate, University of Denver, School of Professional Psychology, Denver, Colorado; Clinical psychology intern, Napa State Hospital, Napa, California

William R. Boyd, Jr., M.S.
Doctoral candidate, The Fielding Institute, Santa Barbara, California; Private practice and training, SteppingStone Psychological Services, Dayton, Tennessee

Ralph M. Daniel, Ph.D.
Director of Santa Barbara Ericksonian Lectures; Private practice, Santa Barbara, California

Hugh Gunnison, Ed.D.
Coordinator, Graduate Program in Counseling and Human Development, St. Lawrence University, Canton, New York

Ronald A. Havens, Ph.D.
Private practice and training; Associate Professor of Psychology, Sangamon State University, Springfield, Illinois

Carol J. Kershaw, Ed.D.
Psychologist in private practice and training, Institute for Family Psychology; Co-Director, Milton H. Erickson Institute of Central Texas, Houston, Texas

Stephen R. Lankton, M.S.W.
Private practice and training; Faculty, Department of Psychology, University of West Florida, Pensacola, Florida

William J. Matthews, Ph.D.
Assistant Professor, Counseling Psychology Program, School of Education, University of Massachusetts, Amherst, Massachusetts

Ernest Lawrence Rossi, Ph.D.
Clinical psychologist in private practice, Los Angeles, California; Editor of the four volumes of *The Collected Works of Milton H. Erickson on Hypnosis;* currently Editor of *Psychological Perspectives,* a semiannual journal of Jungian thought.

Editor's Preface to Monograph No. 2

Central Themes and Principles of Ericksonian Therapy

The *Ericksonian Monographs* was established in 1984 by The Milton H. Erickson Foundation, Inc. as a means to further its aim of bringing the work and influence of Dr. Erickson to an ever-widening professional audience. The *Monographs* offers an ongoing forum for the publication of high quality articles of theory, case material, and research written by eminent professionals who are applying Ericksonian methods and principles in their practice.

This second issue of the *Monographs* goes to press just over a year after the very successful first issue arrived. We are proud to add two new members to the Editorial Board: Kristina K. Erickson, M.D., and William J. Matthews, Ph.D. The theme of this issue, "Central Themes and Principles of Ericksonian Therapy," reflects the authors' desire to discover and add what is essential in Erickson's approach to their therapeutic work. Addressing this theme we have nine articles including techniques, perspectives, and theory.

Several articles provide theoretical foundations and creative ideas for interventions related to the themes. Dr. Ronald Havens' theoretical article emphasizes and explicates an essential principle to Ericksonian therapy —Future Orientation. He demonstrates how therapy ought not attempt to deal with the past but rather should assist clients in creatively operating in the future. Dr. Hugh Gunnison has compared basic similarities in the approaches of Doctors Rogers and Erickson and illustrates commonality regarding their use of the most basic and essential traits of respect and caring. Dr. Ernest Rossi has included "Memory and Hallucination, Part II," underscoring the several definitive elements of Dr. Erickson's trance work relating his early work to modern state-dependent learning theory. Dr. James Allen has provided a theoretical paper on the centrality of the Self in Dr. Erickson's work. Drawing from the work of many Self-theorists and Ericksonian therapists, he makes an important contribution to our understanding of this vital aspect of therapy as well as giving us a new look at some well-known cases.

This issue also contains a number of case studies and case illustrations to further illustrate the theme. Stephen Lankton's article on the Scramble Technique answers the many requests to put into print this technique for symptom grading and confusion. Both theory and transcripts are included for clarity. Carol Kershaw has provided a case study of the brief treatment of childhood asthma with a systemic approach. She paints a crystal-clear portrait of the recursive and interlocking dynamics within a family system. Dr. William Matthews and Dr. Ralph Daniel have authored a case dealing with pain control that engages both spouses in the hypnotic treatment. The result is an attempt to alter the systemic effect created by communication between the partners about the pain as well as other perceptions and sensations related to pain control.

Case studies by Eric Aronson display an Ericksonian approach to shyness and provide a most lucid and complete examination of the phenomena of shyness from several therapeutic perspectives. Dr. William Boyd has applied the principles of Ambiguous Function Assignment to several cases with some very interesting results. He presents the Lanktons' theory for this class of assignments and the creative use of it in several of his cases.

We have, in summary, an issue regarding the application of central themes and underlying principles in Ericksonian therapy—a rich compendium of research and techniques for readers.

Gulf Breeze, Florida   Stephen R. Lankton
December, 1986

Central Themes and Principles of Ericksonian Therapy

The Future Orientation
of Milton H. Erickson:
A Fundamental Perspective
for Brief Therapy

Ronald A. Havens, Ph.D.

Milton H. Erickson initiated profound changes in individuals and families with brief but intense interventions. A basic element of his perspective which enabled him to devise therapeutic strategies rapidly and accomplish major changes was his ability to orient himself and his clients toward the future. This paper describes Erickson's future orientation and outlines the implications of this orientation for the use of various Ericksonian techniques such as metaphors, anecdotes, and a hypnotic technique he called "pseudo-orientation in time."

Milton H. Erickson was raised in a small farming community in a rural section of Wisconsin. The significance of this seemingly trivial piece of background information might have escaped my attention completely if Erickson himself had not emphasized and explained it.

During one of his professional teaching seminars in his home, Erickson raised the issue of his country background. As quoted by Zeig (1980), he stated:

> The country child is oriented to getting up at sunrise and working all summer long until after sundown and always working with a view toward the future. You plant things; you wait for them to grow; and you harvest them. Everything you do on the farm is oriented toward the future. (p. 231)

Address reprint requests to: Ronald A. Havens, Ph.D., Associate Professor of Psychology, Sangamon State University, Springfield, IL 62708.

After telling several related anecdotes about his childhood and about some of his patients, Erickson noted:

> Insight into the past may be somewhat educational. But insight into the past isn't going to change the past. If you were jealous of your mother, it is always going to be a fact that you *were* jealous of her. If you were unduly fixated on your mother, it is always going to be the fact. You may have insight, but it doesn't change the fact. Your patient has to live in accord with things of today. So you orient your therapy to the patient living today and tomorrow, and hopefully next week and next year. (Zeig, 1980, p. 269)

In other words, you must orient your patients toward the future, not toward the past.

This was not the only occasion when Erickson emphasized the importance of a future orientation to the practice of effective therapy. He mentioned it frequently throughout his career and demonstrated it blatantly whenever he worked with a patient.

It is the purpose of this paper to suggest that almost all of Erickson's interventions can be understood as efforts to provide his patients with a therapeutic orientation toward the future. It also is the purpose of this paper to suggest that the ability to conduct effective therapy with individuals, couples, or families will improve significantly as the therapist shifts more fully into a future orientation.

The Past Versus the Future

A majority of therapists have been trained to approach patients from a historical explanatory perspective. The typical goal or purpose of the therapy is to identify the etiology of present problems or dynamics with the implicit assumption that once a patient understands what went wrong, he or she will know how to fix it.

This conceptual orientation is so ingrained in therapeutic folklore that patients bring it with them into the therapist's office. All therapists have encountered individuals, couples, or families who, left to their own devices, would spend hour after hour dredging up every unpleasant episode they can remember in an effort to account for their present situation. In some instances this chronic review of the past amounts to little more than an attempt to shift the burden of responsibility or blame for existing problems onto someone else. But even when it is a genuine effort to accurately assess the etiology and dynamics of an unpleasant situation, the fact remains that such understanding does not produce change.

The purpose of brief therapy is to produce rapid change, not self-understanding; and change is, by necessity, a future event. The focus in brief therapy, therefore, must be upon the future and away from the past.

Patients and the Past

This is not meant to imply that Erickson had no concern for a patient's past at all. He maintained that the therapist needed to be aware of the patient's past but that the patient had no such need. For example, in 1954, he said: "It is essential that the therapist understand it [the patient's past] as fully as possible but without compelling the patient to achieve the same degree of special erudition" (Erickson, 1954, p. 128).

Erickson's prescription for patients with respect to the past is more strikingly conveyed by the following comment to one of his patients: "Well, the deed is done and cannot be undone, so let the dead past bury its dead" (Erickson, 1980, Vol. 1, p. 325).

The full significance of this statement was brought home to me by an incest and child abuse victim. She was undergoing a great deal of emotional distress as a result of her memories of her abusive childhood. After discussing her situation briefly she looked at me and said, "To be honest, I would just as soon forget all about it. It doesn't do me any good to remember how I felt as a child. It just hurts."

This seemed like a valid observation and a reasonable request. Accordingly, during hypnotic trance she was told to say goodbye to that child and to experience an emotional detachment from her. She cried for several minutes and then said she was sorry she had to leave her back there in that mess but that there was nothing she could do for her now. She then said that she felt a great sense of relief and asked to be awakened. After reorienting to the office she stated that she felt like now she could get on with her life. She had "let the dead past bury its dead" and continues to be much better off for it. Since that time similar procedures have been used with other incest and abuse victims with consistently beneficial results.

Therapists and the Past

Although Erickson did not advocate insight into the past for patients, he did maintain that therapists should understand thoroughly their patients' pasts. He almost invariably gathered basic background information such as age, education, marital status, number of children, siblings' names and ages, and rural or urban background. He also often explored the etiology of a presenting problem via discussion or hypnosis. But when he did so it was with an eye toward the patient's possible future and not with the goal of providing special insights into the past. As he noted: "It is out of the patient's past that better and more adequate ways are derived to help the patient live his future" (Erickson, 1954, p. 128).

Erickson was interested in the past only to the extent that it offered him a basis for propelling his patients into a better future. What Erickson looked for as he examined his patients' histories were the perspectives, motivations, learnings, and potentials they brought with them into the office. He focused upon their attributes and resources rather than their diagnoses or upon complex theoretical analyses of their intrapsychic or interpersonal backgrounds.

For example, a relatively informal review of Erickson's published descriptions of his patients by Havens and Walters (1986) found that 78% of the time he used only common, everyday descriptive terms. Furthermore, of 153 cases reviewed, theoretical constructs were employed descriptively in only 3%, diagnostic terms in only 10%, but common everyday terms in 97%. This data clearly indicate that Erickson observed his patients from a perspective that was not dominated by theoretical constructs or diagnostic labels. Instead he observed in a straightforward manner searching for the basic orientations, abilities, and resources of his patients.

Erickson wanted to find out how his patients related to the world around them—what motivated them, what interested them, what pleased them, what guided their decisions, and what influenced their expectations. He wanted to know if their orientation was dominated by urban, rural, or ethnic upbringing, a prudish background, level of education, vocation, role as parent, visual versus aural perceptual orientation, parental injunctions, and so forth.

Erickson wanted to know what colored his patients' basic orientations because he wanted to be able to communicate with them in a language or style that was consistent with that orientation. If a patient speaks only Spanish, you must speak to that patient in Spanish if you hope to influence his or her future. If a patient is a teacher, then examples appropriate to a teacher's orientation can be useful. If a patient is a prude, then that prudish orientation can enable the therapist to communicate in ways that capture attention.

Erickson also wanted to know what skills, experiences, abilities, beliefs, and motivations his patients brought into his office because they were the source of the resources he would teach them to use to build better futures. He spoke to them in a language he knew they would understand and he utilized that communication to help them use their own inner resources to do things differently. His understanding of their past enabled him to do these things effectively.

A thorough discussion of the assessment of a patient's present orientation and resources is beyond the scope of this paper. Characteristically, Erickson himself provided little clarification of the process. However, the interested reader is referred to Lankton and Lankton (1983) for a useful discussion. For present purposes, this basic discussion is sufficient.

Future Orientation Techniques

If Erickson's instructions for assessing a patient's present orientation were cryptic or indirect, his instructions for using that information to affect a patient's future were even more puzzling. For example, in Zeig (1980) Erickson interjects between anecdotes: "And so when you look at a patient, when you listen to a patient, find out what his orientation is. Then try to give him some idea of how to orient himself" (p. 253).

"Try to give him some idea of how to orient himself." The ambiguity underlying this simple directive is astounding and yet it captures the essence of Erickson's approach to psychotherapy. Virtually every technique he employed was designed to "try to give him some idea of how to orient himself." Thus, perhaps we should say that Erickson taught by example, not by direct instruction, how to use the orientation colored by a patient's past to help that individual acquire better and more adequate ways to live his or her future. A review of a few of his case histories, therefore, should convey the basic structure and purpose of his future-oriented approach to therapy.

Pseudo-Orientation in Time

A straightforward demonstration of Erickson's future orientation in therapy is his use of a hypnotic technique he discussed in an article entitled "Pseudo-Orientation in Time as a Hypnotherapeutic Procedure" (Erickson, 1954). In this article Erickson presents five case histories. Each is a truly dramatic example of the potency of a future-oriented approach to therapy.

Essentially the same technique was used with each patient. During trance they were told to experience themselves or an image of themselves at some unspecified time in the near future when therapy had concluded satisfactorily. They were then asked to "remember" and review, from their future vantage point, the events that had led to this desirable outcome. After an extensive review of these fantasized accomplishments the patients usually were told to forget everything that had happened during trance and were awakened.

Erickson's report of subsequent events has an almost spooky quality to it. In one case, a man viewed future scenes of himself asking his boss for a raise, dating a woman, buying a new suit, having his car painted, and giving a speech to a group of men. When Erickson originally agreed to see him he had held a minor clerical position, had no friends, lived in a "wretched" rooming house, engaged in no form of recreation, and had spent much of the past three years visiting his physician with innumerable somatic complaints. Within eight weeks of his pseudo-orientation in time experience he had requested and received a raise, had his car repainted, bought a new suit, begun dating a secretary he met at a dance, moved to a new apartment, given a speech to the Young Businessmen's Club, and, in general, had turned his life around. The parallels between what he fantasized himself doing to effect his recovery and what he actually ended up doing were obvious, except that he had no memory of his fantasies and no awareness that he was carrying out the future he had already imagined for himself!

A similar process was used with similar results with an unhappy woman who had been unable to move out of her parents' home, refused to accept a promotion at work, avoided all social activities, and generally seemed unable to do anything she said she wanted to do. During hypnosis this woman was asked to hallucinate a crystal ball image of herself happily engaging in some future activity. She visualized herself at the upcoming wedding of a friend, wearing a beautiful dress, talking happily with others, dancing with several men, and even named the man who was asking her for a date. She was awakened with amnesia for this entire episode.

Three months later, several days after the actual wedding, she entered Erickson's office without an appointment to report her progress. She had made her own dress, had become involved in shopping for wedding presents with friends, had arranged several showers for the bride, had happily danced with a number of men at the reception, and had been asked out on a date by the man she named originally. She also had accepted a promotion at work so that she would have the money for these preparations and had moved into an apartment closer to her office to avoid losing shopping and wedding preparation time on the long drive to her parents' home. She apparently had no awareness that these activities had effected a "cure," nor that they were related to her hypnosis session.

Following Erickson's lead, I have oriented many patients into their own desirable futures with almost equally impressive results. A detailed description of one case is available in my article, "Posthypnotic Predetermination of Therapeutic Progress" (Havens, 1986). Apparently, once people have envisioned a pathway into a desirable future and have imagined themselves carrying out the necessary steps, there is a remarkable tendency to actually respond to events in a manner consistent with these outcomes. Or, as Erickson described it: "Deeds are the offspring of hope and expectancy" (Erickson, 1954, p. 261).

Metaphors and Anecdotes

Much has been written about Erickson's use of metaphors and anecdotes during the therapeutic process. Rosen (1982) referred to Erickson's stories as "teaching tales" and this seems an appropriate description. But Erickson's stories and metaphors typically were designed to do more than make a point or present a moral. They were designed to give patients instructions regarding new or better orientations, new ways to solve problems, or new ways to lead their lives.

Change-oriented therapists usually have no difficulty coming up with better ways for their patients to think or to live in the future. The problem is that it rarely does any good to tell a patient these ideas. Patients tend to reject direct suggestions, argue that they cannot change, and so forth. For this reason, Erickson frequently presented his directions for better living indirectly embedded within anecdotes and metaphors and often used a trance to reduce even further a patient's resistance.

The power and potential of metaphors and anecdotes are that they enable the therapist to tell a patient indirectly how to do things differently in the future. When this future-oriented message is embedded in a story, both the therapist and the patient can *pretend* that the therapist is not telling the patient what to think or do. This is especially true when the patient is in a trance. As a result, patients end up carrying out the implied suggestion, but with little or no conscious recognition that they are doing what they were told to do.

An effective demonstration of this process is contained in Erickson's description of a hypnotic psychotherapy session he conducted in front of an audience of psychiatrists with a severely depressed, reportedly suicidal student nurse named Betty (cf. Zeig, 1980, pp. 148-153). As far as the audience knew he was merely demonstrating various hypnotic phenomena such as time distortion, hallucinations, and so forth. But while Erickson had Betty hallucinate trips to the arboretum, the zoo, and the beach, he told her about the changes in the seasons, the production of fruit and seeds, the planting process, the birth process, migrations of fish, mammals, and birds, the many generations of people who had enjoyed the beach, and the constant changes in the ocean.

Betty vanished the next day. Police were called in but no trace was found. Many people assumed Erickson's session with her had somehow precipitated her suicide.

Sixteen years later Betty called Erickson and told him that the evening of her session with him she had gone to the Naval Recruiting Station and demanded immediate induction into the Nursing Corps. She served two enlistments, was discharged in Florida where she got a job in a hospital, met and married a retired officer, and subsequently had five children. It is difficult to imagine a more direct response to a discussion of life in the future, of migration, and of the ocean. Had Erickson simply told her directly that she was obviously unhappy in her present life, that actually there was much to look forward to in the future and that she should find some way to travel and enjoy herself, it is possible she would have taken his comments and advice just as seriously, but it is doubtful.

One of Erickson's patients described the process this way:

> I tell him how I'm feeling, and he sits there for a few minutes, and taking my case in relation with an anecdote, happening, things that have happened to his friends, his family, to himself. You know, he winds them all up together, and the first thing you know lo and behold, I find out he's talking about me all the time. (Haley, 1985, Vol. 1, p. 317)

When Erickson began telling an anecdote or a metaphor, he made certain that his patients didn't know he was talking about them, instructing them. But, as he noted: "Then when I see them beginning to apply it to themselves, and when I see them stepping over and joining me, then I can shift explicitly to them" (Haley, 1985, Vol. 1., p. 324).

The explicit point of this process for Erickson was to give his patients a new orientation to their future, to push them to use their abilities and potentials to accomplish the right goal at the right time. He always had his eye on their future and his anecdotes and metaphors provided the pathway into that future.

Describing Future Consequences

At times patients are determined to do something inappropriate or unwise, though they are convinced that their intentions are good and the outcome will be desirable. Erickson dealt with this situation by accepting their intentions and praising them for being willing to accept the overlooked negative consequences, which he then described in detail.

Erickson did not try to argue patients out of doing something that they had their minds set on doing. He recognized that such an approach would merely make people defend their decision and become more firmly committed to it.

He also recognized that once people experience a negative view of a future course of action, they will tend to avoid it. The underlying principle is identical to that employed in the "pseudo-orientation in time" technique described previously. People tend automatically to behave in accord with their underlying view or expectations of the future. If they can imagine a future course of action that will have beneficial consequences, that is what they will tend to do. If they are led to view a course of action as having negative consequences, they will find a reason to avoid it.

An interesting example of this technique is provided by Haley (1973, pp. 280-282). The presenting problem involved the possessive, oversolicitous parents of a young woman who were insisting that their daughter and son-in-law live with them after their marriage. The parents even had built an addition to their house for that purpose. Erickson agreed to see the parents during which time he praised their willingness to serve as baby-sitters at any time in the future, to enjoy the baby crying, and, in general, to sacrifice their present ways of living. After his portrayal of the future to which they could look forward if their daughter actually moved into the new addition, the parents gradually shifted their position and ended up renting the space to a mature, quiet person. Erickson altered their perception of the future by attaching negative outcomes to their plans, not by debating the merits of them.

This approach can be used to influence long-term adjustments to life in addition to stimulating resolutions of short-term problems. For example, many patients seem to ignore or overlook a basic consequence of being alive, that is, the potential for being dead at any moment. Their failure to pay attention to this fact often leads them to make poor decisions, to constantly postpone pleasures, and to be willing to waste a remarkable amount of time and energy.

As Erickson once observed:

> We all start dying when we are born. Some of us are faster than others. Why not live and enjoy, because you can wake up dead. You won't know about it. But somebody else will worry then. Until that time—enjoy life. (Zeig, 1980, p. 269)

Whenever I see a patient who has failed to incorporate this fact, I tell them about a program I saw on the Public Broadcasting System that showed a man who invested his entire life working, saving money, and planning to finally enjoy himself after his retirement. Two months after he retired he was told he had terminal cancer and had only a few weeks to live. I then praise the patients for having the courage to risk a similar outcome and ask them to list all of the things they would do differently if they knew they only had a short time to live. After they have reviewed this list, I again tell them how impressed I am with their willingness to risk missing out on so many wonderful experiences and express my sincere wish that they will live long enough to avoid the devastating experience of the man on PBS. Few people fail to make major adjustments in their long-term approach to life following such a frightening presentation of the potential consequences of their present attitudes.

Prescribing Behavior Changes

Unless people begin thinking and/or behaving differently, the future will be a perpetuation of the past. Erickson recognized this and also recognized that even a small, seemingly innocuous or insignificant change in relation to the problem would precipitate a growing sequence of changes in the future. As he said on more than one occasion: "Therapy is often a matter of tipping the first domino" (Rossi, 1973, p. 14).

Erickson wanted his patients to do something different, preferably something that violated their rigidities, phobias, or destructive interpersonal relationship patterns. His goal was to precipitate a more major change in the future. Often he accomplished this by straightforwardly instructing his patients to do something they had never done before or to do something in a manner they had never done before. He always made sure that his assignment was something the patient could do and would do. Usually it was just a minor variation on an existing behavior pattern. At times, however, he had people perform a totally unrelated act in a specific way because he wanted them to have an opportunity to respond in a new way to a metaphorical or symbolic representation of their problem. He maintained that once they had responded to the metaphorical representation in a new way, they would be more likely to respond to the actual problem situation in that new manner.

An example of an assignment of a variation on an old way of handling a problem area is contained in his treatment of a couple whose problem involved a restaurant they had run together for many years (Haley, 1973, p. 225). The wife argued that the husband should be able to manage the business while she stayed home. The husband argued that he would like to do so except she was always there nagging him and criticizing everything he did. The wife, of course, felt she had to be there or the place would fall apart.

Erickson made a small change in their routine that solved the problem entirely. He told the wife that she should see to it that the husband got to the restaurant half an hour before she did, not at the same time. That single alteration had reverberating consequences. Since the husband arrived first, he was in charge. By the time the wife showed up, everything was in motion and there was nothing for her to do. She began arriving later and later and the now unmolested husband ran the business quite effectively from then on. Both were pleased!

Similar examples abound in the literature on Erickson's work. A small change in a pattern of behavior leads automatically to other changes in the future.

Summary

The future-oriented Ericksonian clinician does not bother explaining or describing to patients how or why the present situation evolved. Although the Ericksonian clinician should understand the developmental dynamics of the patient's past and should incorporate that understanding into the treatment plan, patients do not necessarily need to know how they got where they are in order to change.

Instead, the future-oriented therapist gives patients a new way of thinking about their future or a new way of doing things in the future. The array of techniques devised by Erickson to accomplish this goal includes the simple prescription of a small change in the way the problem is currently handled, the presentation in a manner the patient must accept of the negative future consequences of a present course of action, the indirect presentation of suggested alterations in behavior by embedding them within a metaphor or anecdote, and the use of trance to enable the patient to "rehearse" a more productive future. In these and other ways, Erickson planted seeds and waited for them to grow.

An increasing numbers of therapists follow the recommendation of this farm boy from rural Wisconsin and "always work with a view toward the future," it is likely that new and even more effective techniques will be developed. The future of brief therapy seems promising indeed.

References

Erickson, M. (1954). Pseudo-orientation in time as a hypnotherapeutic procedure, *Journal of Clinical and Experimental Hypnosis, 2*, 261-283.

Erickson, M. (1980). Resistant patients. In E. Rossi (Ed.), *The collected papers of Milton H. Erickson on hypnosis.* (Vol. 1, pp. 299-330). New York: Irvington.

Haley, J. (1973). *Uncommon therapy.* New York: Norton.

Haley, J. (1985). *Conversations with Milton H. Erickson* (Vol. 1), New York: Triangle Press.

Havens, R. (1986). Posthypnotic predetermination of therapeutic progress. *American Journal of Clinical Hypnosis, 4,* 258-262.

Havens, R., & Walters, C. (1986). Empirical analysis of terms used by Milton H. Erickson to describe patients. Paper presented at *Midwest Psychological Association Convention*, Chicago, IL.

Lankton, S. R., & Lankton, C. H. (1983). *The Answer within: A clinical framework of Ericksonian hypnotherapy.* New York: Brunner/Mazel.

Rosen, S. (1982). *My voice will go with you: The teaching tales of Milton H. Erickson.* New York: Norton.

Rossi, E. (1973). Psychological shocks and creative moments in therapy. *American Journal of Clinical Hypnosis, 16,* 9-22.

Zeig, J. (1980). *A teaching seminar with Milton H. Erickson.* New York: Brunner/ Mazel.

Comparisons of Values and Beliefs of M. H. Erickson's Utilization Approach and C. R. Rogers' Person-Centered Approach

Hugh Gunnison, Ed.D.

This paper attempts to examine several fundamental beliefs and assumptions regarding the human condition as set forth in the works of Milton H. Erickson and Carl R. Rogers. Beginning students in counseling and psychotherapy often become overly enthralled with techniques and strategies to the exclusion of beliefs and philosophic assumptions undergirding their methods. It seems safe to say that M. H. Erickson and C. R. Rogers have become giants in their related fields. While vast differences in techniques and strategies remain, this paper will argue that a common thread of values and beliefs regarding human beings weaves itself throughout the work and writings of both men.

Our strategies, our interventions, and our overall approaches belie our fundamental attitudes and beliefs regarding the "nature of man." If I believe in my clients' abilities to take responsibility, to trust in their vast resources, learnings, and experiences, and in their potential to choose, then I will tend to assume an approach in counseling or therapy congruent with these beliefs.

Address reprint requests to: Hugh Gunnison, Ed.D., Department of Education, St. Lawrence University, Canton, NY 13617.

Many years ago, as a hospital corpsman in the military service, I studied traditional hypnosis with a psychiatrist. The process involved talking in a low monotonous voice and continually repeating suggestions (which seemed more like condescending commands), all the while swinging an object (preferably shiny) in front of the subject's eyes. I grew increasingly disenchanted and uncomfortable. I have come to see this earlier form of hypnosis, in some respects, as demeaning and disrespectful to the client. The hypnotist became the authority rarely taking into consideration the perceptual field and uniqueness of the client. It seemed as if the hypnotist operated from his or her map and expected the client to obey. In reaction, I became drawn to the work of Carl Rogers. His work represented the exact opposite: It represented caring, respect, and equality for clients. Later, a reexamination of hypnosis came through the works of Milton H. Erickson. Although the subject matter still concerned the use of hypnosis, clients were treated from value and belief systems entirely different from those to which I had previously been exposed. Erickson's work came as a breath of fresh air and the similarities between his utilization approach and Rogers' person-centered approach became evident to me.* These observations led me to writing about these parallels (Gunnison, 1985).

Dr. Rogers wrote a response to that earlier paper I had written on the parallels between Erickson and his own work (Gunnison, 1985): "I am profoundly impressed by the similarities that Gunnison found between my work and that of Milton Erickson" (Rogers, 1985, p. 565).

Rogers (1985) claims little personal acquaintance with Dr. Erickson except slightly as undergraduates at the University of Wisconsin. He has not read any appreciable proportion of Erickson's writings and to his knowledge Erickson did not have personal contact or acquaintance with Rogers' writings. He explained, "I mention these things to indicate that whatever similarities exist developed quite independently—certainly not out of close contact or thorough knowledge of each other's writings. The similarities are therefore real and not simply derivative" (Rogers, 1985, p. 565).

This paper will attempt to examine those commonalities as well as include Rogers' (1985, 1986) reactions. This comparison underscores parallels in 10 areas. These consist of: the magnitude of their impact on the field of psychotherapy; their personal history and development of values; person-centeredness; the unconscious; nonreliance on theory; the self as a

---

*Araoz (1985) for some time has stressed a similar linkage in his New Hypnosis. It seems crucial and salient that theorists are beginning to synthesize more, rather than construct distancing and isolated maps.

tool; the importance of empathy and rapport; communication and intuition; caring and respect for the client; and the use of metaphors to retrieve therapeutic resources.

The Magnitude of Their Impact on Psychotherapy

As I started learning about the processes of Erickson's endeavors, I became impressed by his daring individuality. It seemed to me that Erickson's work existed as an exquisite example of experiential and personal learning. His skills, breadth of knowledge, his sensitive astuteness, and creativity resulted in his being called Mr. Hypnosis (Weitzenhoffer, 1976). He emerged as the founding leader and first president of the American Society for Clinical Hypnosis and the founder and editor of its journal.

It seemed that he could put conventional theories aside and begin creating a model of human internal processing through sensitive and astute observation both of self and others. His was a radical stance, and it seems that Rogers moved in a parallel direction. Both might appear as rebels in their profession because of their unique beliefs and methods of approaching the therapeutic process. Each has shared a similar curiosity and Rogers describes it as the immediate experience of the observer. For Rogers (1980) the starting point of science occurs at the moment of concentrated and focused observation. Erickson probably could not have agreed more wholeheartedly.

Rogers has gained a status similar to that of Erickson. Out of his thinking, writing, and research a "school" within psychology emerged, despite his wishes to the contrary. Both Rogers and Erickson decried the rigidification and channeling resulting from "theoretical schools." Neither sought to be a leader-guru of a movement nor desired to found a "school" of therapy.

Smith (1982) surveyed practicing psychologists requesting that they list the names of those who had influenced them the most and Carl Rogers' name led the list. Zeig (1980) wrote that "It is not hyperbole to state that history will demonstrate that what Freud contributed to the theory of psychotherapy, Erickson will be known as contributing to the practice of psychotherapy" (p. xix). The Lanktons (Lankton & Lankton, 1983) use another analogy, " . . . Erickson's influence is thought by many to equal Freud's. Whereas Freud can be thought of as the Einstein of theory, Erickson will likely be acknowledged as the Einstein of intervention" (p. 6). And Zeig (1985b) reported that "Ericksonian methods are probably the fastest growing field of psychotherapy in the western world" (p. 31).

Personal History and Development of Values

"The child is father of the man" wrote the poet laureate William Wordsworth, and the childhood experiences of Erickson and Rogers are inextricably intertwined with the shaping and the creation of the histories of their values. Each grew up on a farm in a rural community. Each became indelibly infused by the growth processes they witnessed daily "and the experiences that permeated their values—the optimistic and positive joy in life and in the simple everchanging world around them. Both emphasized and sensed the uniqueness of each living thing and prized above all those differences" (Gunnison, 1985, p. 563).

Although Erickson was struck by polio in adolescence, few may be aware that as a young child Rogers was seriously ill as well. He tells how, "As a boy I was rather sickly and my parents have told me that it was predicted I would die young" (Rogers, 1980, p. 89). Viktor Frankl (1965) argued that suffering can stretch, enrich, and motivate the human, and, perhaps, the early years of pain and suffering somehow deepened Erickson's and Rogers' values of sensitivity and appreciation of growth and of change. These life experiences may have led to the development of those values which other authors have found noteworthy.

> Milton Erickson had a clearly defined value system. Evident in his work are: the strength of his convictions about the integrity of each human being; the importance of the family; the necessity of strong and close relationships with others; and the positive internal potentials of each person. (Yapko, 1985, p. 280)

The same thing could have been said of Rogers. "Values have been described as an enduring filter through which subjective experience is created, interpreted, and reacted to" (Yapko, 1985, p. 273). "The values of *the man Erickson* [*Rogers*] underlie *the psychiatrist Erickson* [psychologist Rogers]" [italics and brackets added] (Yapko, 1985, p. 268).

Patient-Person-Centeredness

The utilization approach of Erickson has been described as " . . . *patient centered* and highly dependent on the momentary needs of the individual" [italics added] (Erickson & Rossi, 1979, p. 14). Like Erickson, Rogers had a realistic, yet positive and optimistic view of the potentials of the human being. He (Rogers, 1980) described the two major tenets of a person-centered approach.

... Individuals have within themselves vast resources for self-understanding and for altering their self-concepts, basic attitudes and self-directed behavior; these resources can be tapped if a definable climate of facilitative psychological attitudes can be provided. (p. 115)

I wonder how Erickson might have reacted to this sentence noting the usage of "resources," "altering self-concept," "attitudes and behavior," as well as the idea of these "resources facilitating" growth and change? We will never know, but I think I do.

At first, Rogers' nondirective stance and Erickson's directive approach may appear as diametric opposites. However, upon further consideration this contradiction dissolves and probably becomes a difference more of degree than of kind. Rogers became chained to "nondirective" and because of the many misunderstandings he tried to struggle free. By "nondirective" he simply meant not interpreting, advising, guiding, or explaining, but rather trusting the person's actualizing tendency to emerge.

Rogers (1977) soon realized that his presence in the therapeutic relationship had a powerful impact and had certain "directive" results. Direction and manipulation can be perceived as the heart of communication.

Manipulation has a negative connotation. However, as communication analysts such as Watzlawick point out, it is impossible not to manipulate [direct]. Interpersonal exchange is predicated on manipulation. Manipulation is unavoidable; the issue is how to manipulate constructively and therapeutically. (Zeig, 1985b, p. xv)

And while Erickson directed (manipulated), he avoided lecturing or interpreting, and the guiding he did, invariably moved the patient inward.

As with the person-centered approach of Rogers, Erickson's utilization approach *centered* on the patient utilizing and activating unconscious resources and learnings already within rather than imposing from without (Erickson, Rossi, & Rossi, 1976). Erickson wrote, "Who is the important person in a therapeutic situation? Is it the therapist? ... I don't think the therapist is *the* important person; I think the patient is *the* important person in this situation. I think, too, that the patient should be given the opportunity to dominate in any way ... (Rossi, 1980, Vol. 4, p. 78). "Utilization" basically says that techniques are best derived from the patient, not from the therapist.... His orientation was to strengthen what is right with the patient rather than analyzing deficits" (Zeig, 1985b, pp. 37-38).

In a dialogue with Erickson, Rossi (Erickson, Rossi, & Rossi, 1976) observed that: "Patients keep pulling at the therapist for the cure, the magic, the change, rather than looking at themselves as the change agent. You are continually putting the responsibility for change back on the patient." Erickson replied: "On to them always" (p. 27). And I cannot imagine Rogers disagreeing with any of this.

The Client's Inner Motivation

Rogers and Erickson in their words and actions both emphasized the internal motivation and processing within people: Rogers in his growth-formative tendency and Erickson in his view of the unconscious. Both Erickson and Rogers believed in the individual's potential toward growth. Rogers (1961) stated it explicitly:

> There is one central source of energy in the human organism. This source is a trustworthy function of the whole system rather than of some portion of it; it is most simply conceptualized as a tendency toward fulfillment, toward ac-tualization, involving not only the maintenance but also the enhancement of the organism. (p. 123)

This growth tendency came to be labeled as the formative tendency (Rogers, 1978), or, as Szent-Gyoergyi (1974), a Nobel prize winning biologist, put it, the principle of "syntropy." Since entropy represents the natural tendency of inorganic and organic systems to gradually disin-tegrate as a vast machine slowly runs down, syntropy or the growing en-hancing process becomes equally as important. Erickson, it appears, assigned syntropy, among other processes, to the unconscious and spoke of "the wisdom of the unconscious" (Rosen, 1982b). How interesting and how analogous Rogers' (1961, 1978) phrase, "the wisdom of the organism," becomes. In fact, Rogers (1986) in a more recent article agrees, "When I look at Erickson's work, I find that he also seems to trust this directional aspect in the person. . . . Both of us find that we can rely, in a very primary way, on the wisdom of the organism" (p. 128).

The Unconscious

Beahrs (1982) discussed Erickson's unconscious not as the fearful, teeming caldron of untamed energy of Freud, but rather as a source for growth, as a repository of all past learning and experiences. Erickson further elaborated, "In hypnosis we utilize the unconscious mind. What do I mean by the unconscious mind? I mean the back of the mind, the reservoir of learning. The unconscious mind constitutes a storehouse"

(Rossi, Vol. 3, 1980, p. 27). Erickson and Rossi discuss another dimension of the unconscious (Rossi, Vol. 1, 1980):

> *Rossi:* You really believe in a creative unconscious?
> *Erickson:* I believe in a different level of awareness.
> *Rossi:* So we could say the unconscious is a metaphor for another level of awareness, a meta-level?
> *Erickson:* I can walk down the street and not have to pay attention to the stop light or the curb. I can climb Squaw Peak and I don't have to figure out each step.
> *Rossi:* Those things are being handled by other levels of awareness. (pp. 119-120)

Sacerdote (1982) expanded on this and wrote of Erickson's concept of the unconscious as being closer to Jung's *archetype*, the unconscious having "attributes of basic wisdom which include the capacity of the body's organs and cells for producing physical and mental healing" (p. 341). Gilligan (1982) discussed Erickson's notion that "Unconscious processes can operate in an intelligent, autonomous, and creative fashion.... People have stored in their unconscious all the resources necessary to transform their experience" (p. 89). Thus, the therapeutic task might become one of arranging conditions (climate) and accessing resources that facilitate and elicit this unconscious processing.

We now have a wider and enhanced picture of the unconscious. It emerges as a non-Freudian construct in its definition and becomes more than just a storehouse of memories and experience. In addition, the concept of the unconscious translates and expands to mean creativity and a capacity for inner wisdom and healing. Erickson (Haley, 1967, 1973) saw the unconscious as the core or center of the person (not unlike Rogers' "self") and significantly emphasized the positive power of the unconscious.

Rogers (1985) used the term "nonconscious" which I cannot really see as differing from Erickson's unconscious. Via a biofeedback example, Rogers (1985) writes of an example of the nonconscious mind at work:

> If you ask me to raise the temperature of the middle finger of my right hand, my conscious mind is completely baffled. It cannot possibly do it. Yet if you show me a needle that indicates the temperature of that finger and ask me if I can make it move upward, I find that I can do it. How do I make all the analyses and discriminations necessary to accomplish this end? It is completely inexplicable if we limit ourselves to the conscious mind. But the nonconscious organic mind is quite capable of the task. (pp. 565-566)

Nevertheless, Rogers (1985) seems to say that this form of the nonconscious that he describes differs from Erickson's unconscious in that Erickson's construct "appears to be more similar to my term 'the actualizing tendency.' I suspect, however, that Erickson would have found the concept of the 'nonconscious' mind congenial" (p. 566). I agree and, furthermore, I believe Erickson might have identified with the biofeedback example as well. I feel hardpressed to find any significant difference here. It seems clear to me that when Rogers thinks about moving a needle upward, he alters his state from a conscious level to "another level" in Erickson and Rossi's (Rossi, Vol. 1, 1980) earlier example of the creative unconscious as meta-level; the moving of the needle by "another level of awareness" (pp. 119-120). The moving needle example might also be explained by Sacerdote's (1982) description of Erickson's unconscious as having a kind of basic wisdom and capacity of the body to produce mental and physical healing.

Nonreliance on Theory

Rogers (1959) believed that the best theoretical paper he had written regarding the person-centered approach came to be published by Sigmund Koch in his monumental series *Psychology: A Study of a Science*. Rogers argued that he worked harder on this theoretical formulation than anything he had written before or since. He said, "It is in my estimation, the most rigorously stated theory of the process of change in personality and behavior which has yet been published" (Evans, 1975, p. 135). This paper will not discuss his theory because Rogers, himself, suggests not doing so. In his own words he said, " . . . it is the most thoroughly ignored of anything I have written. This does not particularly distress me, because I believe theories too often become dogma" (Evans, 1975, p. 137).

Although he developed a rigorous theory, Rogers warned repeatedly of the dangers of overtheorizing, that theories can develop into absolute creeds and become highly rigid. He emphasized the importance of setting theory aside and letting the person emerge. In a class discussion at St. Lawrence University in 1978, he urged us to be there fully for our clients and that "the person becomes your theory." He went on to tell us that what he had "ultimately learned about people was from people."

Erickson advised against limiting our approaches because of fealty to a theory, a method, a school, or a mentor. Instead, he suggested that we learn and observe as widely as possible, practicing only those techniques and skills that allow us to express ourselves authentically. In a lecture Erickson reminded the audience, "Remember that whatever way you choose to work must be your own way, because you cannot really imitate someone else. In dealing with the crucial situations of therapy, you must express yourself adequately, not as an imitation" (Haley, 1967, p. 535).

Secter (1982) once queried Erickson as to where and how he obtained his psychiatric knowledge. "From patients," he responded. Erickson felt that theory was restrictive, stifling, and could trap both patient and therapist (Zeig, 1980). Stern (1985) paraphrased the contents of a personal communication from Erickson:

> . . . each patient is unique and no single theory will fit everyone. That is why, he said, he developed a new theory for each person. . . . Erickson knew that the procrustean myth not only referred to someone with a rigid view, but that the result of that rigidity was Procrustes' own demise. Erickson was a modern-day Theseus who took great pleasure in slaying theories in their own procrustean beds. (p. 79)

Erickson wrote, "In therapeutic approaches one must always take into consideration the actual personality of the individual. . . . Therefore, the more fluidity in the hypnotherapist, the more easily you can actually approach the patient" (Rossi, 1980, Vol. 4, p. 78). Erickson emphasized the ideas of flexibility, indirection, permissiveness, and unique differences. How apt all of these terms seem to describe Rogers' description of the effective counselor-therapist.

Rogers (1961) discussed the process of effective counseling as involving "a change in the manner of the client's experiencing . . . a *loosening* of the *cognitive maps* of experience" [italics added] (p. 64). Note Erickson's parallel remarks: "Patients have problems because their conscious programming has too severely limited their capacities. The solution is to help them break through the limitations of their conscious attitudes to free their unconscious potential for problem solving" (Erickson et al., 1976, p. 18).

The Self as a Tool

When Rogers proposed the growth principle he spent many years studying the therapeutic climate that elicited this growth process. He approached "the phenomena with as few preconceptions as possible, to take a naturalist's observational, descriptive approach. . . . I used myself as a tool" (Rogers, 1961, p. 128).

In his study of hypnosis Erickson also used himself "as a tool," spending countless hours as a young man observing and reflecting on experiences in altered states and learning to relieve his own pain by focusing on relaxation, heaviness, fatigue, dissociation, and so forth (Rossi, 1980); he learned through his own incredible facilities of observation and introspection. "Both he and Rogers were able to look at different ways of 'seeing' themselves, others, and the relativity of different world views" (Gunnison, 1985, p. 562).

The Importance of Empathy and Rapport

Empathy, along with genuineness, unconditional positive regard, and a trust in the potential of the person all together came to represent that "definable" climate so critical in Rogers' work (Rogers, 1957). Empathy becomes a crucial condition. "It means entering the private perceptual world of the other and becoming thoroughly at home in it . . . you lay aside your own views and values in order to enter another's world without prejudice" (Rogers, 1980, pp. 142-143).

Erickson also stressed empathy particularly in the preparation phase of his approach; the most important factor appears as "sound rapport—that is a positive feeling of understanding and mutual regard between therapist and patient" (Erickson & Rossi, 1979, p. 1). Erickson believed that "an attitude of empathy and respect on the part of the therapist is *crucial* to ensure successful change" [italics added] (Erickson & Zeig, 1980, p. 336). He amplified the concept of rapport that develops out of a *genuine* acceptance of the other (Erickson & Rossi, 1979). A powerful kind of empathy developed as Erickson would use the patient's own vocabulary and frames of reference (pacing and matching) to form the interpersonal connection (Grinder & Bandler, 1981). "Meet the client at his or her model of the world" (Lankton & Lankton, 1983, p. 12). It was at this juncture that Rossi commented on the similarity between Erickson's approach and Rogers': "At this level our approach might appear similar to the *nondirective client-centered approach of Rogers (1951)*" [italics added] (Erickson & Rossi, 1979, p. 51).

Communication and Intuition

Genuineness or congruence must stand as another basic condition within the person-centered climate. For if realness does not exist in the relationship, then toxicity and distrust must soon develop. Lankton and Lankton (1983) expanded on counselor-therapist genuineness by adding, "The Ericksonian hypnotherapist must have a personal manner that gives credibility and potency to his or her interventions. It can be called congruity, sincerity, or confidence" (p. 133). Rogers (1986) senses a kind of genuineness in Erickson when he observes,

It seems strikingly clear that for Erickson, too, therapy was a highly personal affair, a deeply involving experience different for each person. He thought about his patients, he reacted to them in very personal ways—challenging, abrupt, patient, soft, hard—always being himself in the interest of the client. He sometimes took individuals into his home, or used pets or told of his own life—doing whatever would keep him in close personal touch. (p. 132)

For the counselor-therapist genuineness means being fully there with the client, sharing clear and transparent communication.

Sometimes a feeling "rises up in me" which seems to have no particular relationship to what is going on. Yet I have learned to accept and trust this feeling by my awareness and to try to communicate it to my client. (Rogers, 1980, p. 14)

This genuineness I suggest is akin to what Erickson would describe as an altered state of consciousness. In fact, Rogers actually uses the words "altered state of consciousness":

I find that when I am closest to my inner, *intuitive self,* when I am somehow in touch with the unknown in me, when perhaps I am in a slightly *altered state of consciousness* in the relationship, that whatever I do seems to be *full of healing.* [italics added] (Rogers, 1985, p. 565)

Rogers (1985) continues:

I have come to value highly these *intuitive* responses. . . . In these moments I am perhaps in a *slightly altered state of consciousness,* in dwelling in the client's world, completely in tune with that world. My *nonconscious* intellect takes over. I know much more than my conscious mind is aware of. [italics added] (p. 565)

The uses of "intuitive," "full of healing," "slightly altered state of consciousness," and "nonconscious" mean to me that Rogers speaks of a process that is at the core of Erickson's work. Erickson so accepted and trusted his own unconscious as well as that of his patients that he became totally in tune with their worlds.

Rossi (1980) reports how Erickson,

. . . is always in complete rapport with the patient. He is never dissociated and out of contact with the patient. Autohypnotic trance usually comes on spontaneously and always enhances his perceptions and relations with the patient. Trance is an intensely focused attention that facilitates his therapeutic work. (Vol. 1, p. 117)

All of this reinforces my conjecture that Rogers and Erickson both utilized the trance state to move more deeply and therapeutically into the encounter. Zeig (1982) felt that Erickson was so "in touch" with his own inner experiences and so *trusted* the "wisdom of *his* unconscious" that he became capable of incredible understandings of his patients' worlds. I believe Rogers is saying essentially the same thing.

Caring and Respect for the Client

Unconditional positive regard came to represent a third core condition. When clients or patients felt appreciated and prized as people, when they felt warmth and trust, and, above all, when they did not feel judged or continually evaluated, change and growing became real possibilities. "It means that he [she] prizes the client, in a nonpossessive way" (Rogers, 1961, p. 62).

Haley (1967) described a similar deep caring in Erickson's work. Erickson spoke of working with a client whom he felt had little chance for successful change. Nevertheless, despite the poor prognosis, Erickson kept the doubts "to himself and he let [the patient] know by manner, tone of voice, by everything said that he [Erickson] was genuinely interested in him, was genuinely desirous of helping him" [brackets added] (Haley, 1967, p. 516). The technical and methodological brilliance of Erickson sometimes can overshadow the therapeutic relationship he emphasized and created with his patients. "It is all too easy to focus on things like Erickson's breathing rate or his use of peripheral vision at the expense of appreciating the intensity of the relationship he had with his patients, which microscopic analysis cannot define any more than one can analyze and define 'love' " (Yapko, 1985, p. 268).

Erickson's writing might summarize the importance of the uniqueness of the person and the therapeutic relationship, "the technique for the induction of hypnotic trances is primarily a function of the interpersonal relationships existing between subject and hypnotist. Hence, hypnotic techniques and procedures should vary according to the subject, circumstances, and the purposes to be served" (Rossi, 1980, Vol. 4, p. 28).

Erickson's basic trust in people came through in his belief and respect in the competence of people to work out things in their own lives. He believed that his patients had the natural desire "to acquire mastery, to obtain understanding, to have fun, to have certainty and to have immediate results" (Lustig, 1982, p. 459).

The Use of Metaphors to Retrieve Therapeutic Resources

One of the strategies of Erickson's indirect utilization approach involved the use of metaphors. These stories and anecdotes served as the tapestry upon which were woven the themes that utilized the patient's experiences, resources, and mental maps. From these metaphors the unconscious mind drew its *own* conclusions and meanings by utilizing its *own* resources stored there in a lifetime of memories of experiences.

Rogers (1985), on the other hand, shared Erickson's liking for the power of metaphor yet differed in its use. He (Rogers, 1985) generally became encouraged when clients would resort to figurative language or metaphor because they often could express themselves much more coherently and deeply than through an exact and literal language:

> So when a client begins to speak of "this heavy bag that I carry around on my back" or speaks of the fear of "walking into darkness—out of light and into the darkness," I feel sure that progress will be made, and I am eager to respond on the metaphorical level....I do use my own metaphors in some intuitive responses, however, and this seems close to Erickson's approach. (Rogers, 1985, p. 566)

Note Rogers' (1961) exquisite story from his youth used to illustrate the growth tendency.

> I remember that in my boyhood, the bin in which we stored our winter's supply of potatoes was in the basement, several feet below a small window. The conditions were unfavorable, but the potatoes would begin to sprout.... But these sad, spindly sprouts would grow two or three feet in length as they reached toward the distant light out of the window. The sprouts were, in their bizarre, futile growth, a sort of desperate expression of the directional tendency.... But under the most adverse circumstances, they were striving to become. Life would not give up, even if it could not flourish. (p. 118)

Erickson's use of anecdotes, puns, metaphors, stories, and jokes has become legendary (Rosen, 1982a). He emphasized:

> ... growth and delight and joy.... Life isn't something you can give an answer to today. You should enjoy the process of waiting, the process of becoming what you are. There is nothing more delightful than planting flower seeds and not knowing what kinds of flowers are going to come up. (Rosen, in Foreword, 1979, p. xii)

Erickson's figurative language suggests open-endedness. It encourages patients to utilize their unconscious mind and search through the vast storehouse of learning, resources, and experiences. Erickson utilizes patients' maps and perceptual fields by the wording and phraseology of his stories that appear relevant and appropriate and thus let the unconscious take over. For example, with the florist, Erickson used a metaphor of the tomato seed in process of becoming a fruit-bearing tomato plant (Haley, 1967). The patient, then, hears the general contextual meaning of a tomato seed in process of becoming at the conscious level, yet the words and phraseology have unique associations that go beyond the general context (Erickson et al., 1976). "In this his interspersal technique, Erickson (1966) inserted words and phrases that indirectly stimulated deeper focusing on the patient's experiences and interests. Through the interspersing of indirect suggestions, the unconscious was put to work" (Gunnison, 1985, p. 563).

Gordon and Myers-Anderson (1981) report a favorite metaphor, a story drawn from Erickson's youth. A riderless horse appeared one day in the Erickson farmyard. No one could identify the owner. Undaunted, Erickson volunteered to find its home and mounted the horse. As he approached the main road he slackened the reins and waited to see in which direction the horse would lead. Erickson intervened only when the horse would wander off the road. After progressing in this fashion for about four miles, sometimes slowly and sometimes quickly, the horse turned into a farmyard. The surprised owner asked Erickson how he knew where the horse belonged. "I didn't know. The horse knew. All I did was keep him on the road" (p. 6). What an extraordinary process description of counseling and therapy! What an exquisite description of the utilization and person-centered approaches!

Conclusion

The discussion in this paper focused on Erickson's work through the lenses of Rogers' person-centered approach. However, the process could easily have been reversed. Gunnison and Renick (1985) describe the subtle and hidden Ericksonian patterns invariably present in much of conventional counseling and therapy. More specifically, Lankton and Lankton (1983) describe and discuss the Ericksonian hypnotic patterns observable in Rogers' work in the film *Gloria*. What appear as two very divergent positions, upon further inspection, evolve into interesting connections and similarities.

While profound differences in approaches exist, Erickson and Rogers had similar beliefs and goals for their clients-patients: the utilizing of their directional tendencies, the evoking of "the wisdom of the unconscious" and "the wisdom of the organism." Rosen (Foreword, 1979) described this as " ... a typical Ericksonian paradox. The master manipulator [facilitator] allows and stimulates the greatest freedom" [brackets added]

(p. xiii). And each did this so genuinely, humanely, and uniquely.

What more fitting way to conclude this writing than to quote from Rogers (1985):

> Although I am sure that there are many differences in Erickson's approach and my own, and perhaps a paper should be written on those, they may not be as important as the similarities. If in our work we both rely on the fundamental directional tendency of the client-patient, if we are intent on permitting the client to choose the directions of his or her life, if we rely on the wisdom of the organism in making such choices, and if we see our role as releasing the client from constraining self-perceptions to become a more complete potential self, then perhaps the differences are not so important as they might seem. (p. 566)

References

Araoz, D.L. (1985). The new hypnosis: The quintessence of client-centeredness. In J.K. Zeig (Ed.), *Ericksonian psychotherapy. Vol. I: Structures* (pp. 256-265). New York: Brunnel/Mazel.

Beahrs, J.O. (1982). Understanding Erickson's approach. In J.K. Zeig (Ed.), *Ericksonian approaches to hypnosis and psychotherapy* (pp. 58-83). New York: Brunner/Mazel.

Erickon, M.H. (1966). The interspersal hypnotic technique for symptom correction and pain control. *American Journal of Clinical Hypnosis, 8,* 198-209.

Erickson, M.H., & Rossi, E. L. (1979). *Hypnotherapy: An exploratory casebook.* New York: John Wiley.

Erickson, M.H., Rossi, E. L., & Rossi, S. I. (1976). *Hypnotic realities: The induction of clinical hypnosis and forms of indirect suggestion.* New York: John Wiley.

Erickson, M.H., & Zeig, J.K. (1980). Symptom prescription for expanding the psychotic's world view. In E. L. Rossi (Ed.), *The collected papers of Milton H. Erickson on hypnosis.* (Vol. 4, pp. 335-337). New York: Irvington.

Evans, R.I. (Ed.). (1975). *Carl Rogers: The man and his ideas.* New York: E.P. Dutton.

Frankl, V. (1965). *The doctor and the soul* (2nd ed.). New York: Knopf.

Gilligan, S.G. (1982). Ericksonian approaches to clinical hypnosis. In J. K. Zeig (Ed.), *Ericksonian approaches to hypnosis and psychotherapy* (pp. 87-103). New York: Brunner/Mazel.

Gordon, D., & Meyers-Anderson, M. (1981). *Phoenix: Therapeutic patterns of Milton H. Erickson.* Cupertino, CA: Meta Publications.

Grinder, J., & Bandler, R. (1981). *Trance-formations: Neurolinguistic programming and the structure of hypnosis.* Moab, UT: Real People Press.

Gunnison, H. (1985). The uniqueness of similarities: Parallels of Milton H. Erickson and Carl Rogers. *Journal of Counseling and Development, 63,* 561-564.

Gunnison, H., & Renick, T.F. (1985). Hidden hypnotic patterns in counseling and supervision. *Counselor Education and Supervision, 25,* 5-11.

Haley, J. (Ed.). (1967). *Advanced techniques of hypnosis and therapy: Selected papers of Milton H. Erickson, M.D.* New York: Grune & Stratton.

Haley, J. (1973). *Uncommon therapy: The psychiatric techniques of Milton H. Erickson, M.D.* New York: W. W. Norton.

Haley, J. (1985). *Conversations with Milton H. Erickson, M. D.* (Vols. 1-3). New York: Triangle Press.

Koch, S. (Ed.). (1959-1963). *Psychology: A study of a science* (Vols. 1-6). New York: McGraw-Hill.

Lankton, S.R., & Lankton, C.H. (1983). *The answer within: A clinical framework of Ericksonian hypnotherapy.* New York: Brunner/Mazel.

Lustig, H.S. (1982). Understanding Erickson and Ericksonian techniques. In J. K. Zeig (Ed.), *Ericksonian approaches to hypnosis and psychotherapy* (pp. 455-461). New York: Brunner/Mazel.

Rogers, C.R. (1951). *Client-centered therapy.* Boston: Houghton-Mifflin.

Rogers, C.R. (1957). The necessary and sufficient conditions of therapeutic personality change. *Journal of Consulting Psychology, 21,* 95-103.

Rogers, C.R. (1959). A theory of therapy, personality and interpersonal relationships, as developed in the client-centered framework. In S. Koch (Ed.), *Psychology: A study of a science. Formulations of the person and the social context* (Vol. 3, pp. 184-256). New York: McGraw-Hill.

Rogers, C.R. (1961). *On becoming a person.* Boston: Houghton-Mifflin.

Rogers, C.R. (1977). *Carl Rogers on personal power.* New York: Dell.

Rogers, C.R. (1978). The formative tendency. *Journal of Humanistic Psychology, 18,* 1-24.

Rogers, C.R. (1980). *A way of being.* Boston: Houghton-Mifflin.

Rogers, C.R. (1985). Reaction to Gunnison's article on the similarities between Erickson and Rogers. *Journal of Counseling and Development, 63,* 565-566.

Rogers, C.R. (1986). Rogers, Kohut, and Erickson—A personal perspective on some similarities and differences. *Person-Centered Review, 1,* 125-140.

Rosen, S. (1979). Foreword. In M. H. Erickson & E. L. Rossi, *Hypnotherapy: An exploratory casebook* (pp. ix-xiii). New York: John Wiley.

Rosen, S. (Ed.). (1982a). *My voice will go with you: The teaching tales of Milton H. Erickson, M.D.* New York: W. W. Norton.

Rosen, S. (1982b). The values and philosophy of Milton H. Erickson. In J. K. Zeig (Ed.), *Ericksonian approaches to hypnosis and psychotherapy* (pp. 462-476). New York: Brunner/Mazel.

Rossi, E.L. (Ed.). (1980). *The collected papers of Milton H. Erickson on hypnosis* (Vols. 1-4). New York: Irvington.

Sacerdote, P. (1982). Erickson's contribution to pain control in cancer. In J. K. Zeig (Ed.), *Ericksonian approaches to hypnosis and psychotherapy* (pp. 336-345). New York: Brunner/Mazel.

Secter, I. (1982). Seminars with Erickson: The early years. In J. K. Zeig (Ed.), *Ericksonian approaches to hypnosis and psychotherapy* (pp. 447-454). New York: Brunner/Mazel.

Smith, D. (1982). Trends in counseling and psychotherapy. *American Psychologist, 379,* 802-809.

Stern, C.R. (1985). There's no theory like no-theory: The Ericksonian approach in perspective. In J. K. Zeig (Ed.), *Ericksonian psychotherapy Vol. I: Structures* (pp. 77-86). New York: Brunner/Mazel.

Szent-Gyoergyi, A. (1974). Drive in living matter to perfect itself. *Synthesis,* Spring, 12-24.

Weitzenhoffer, A.M. (1976). Foreword. In M. H. Erickson, E. L. Rossi, & S.I.

Rossi, *Hypnotic realities: The induction of clinical hypnosis and forms of indirect suggestion* (pp. xiii-xix). New York: John Wiley.

Yapko, M.D. (1985). The Ericksonian hook: Values in Ericksonian approaches. In J.K. Zeig (Ed.), *Ericksonian psychotherapy Vol. 1: Structures* (pp. 266-281). New York: Brunner/Mazel.

Zeig, J.K. (Ed.). (1980). *Teaching seminar with Milton H. Erickson, M.D.* New York: Brunner/Mazel.

Zeig, J.K. (Ed.). (1982). *Ericksonian approaches to hypnosis and psychotherapy.* New York: Brunner/Mazel.

Zeig, J.K. (Ed.). (1985a). *Ericksonian psychotherapy Volume I: Structures.* NewYork: Brunner/Mazel.

Zeig, J.K. (1985b). *Experiencing Erickson: An introduction to the man and his work.* New York: Brunner/Mazel.

Memory and Hallucination (Part II): Updating Classical Association Theory to a State-Dependent Theory of Therapeutic Hypnosis

Ernest Lawrence Rossi, Ph.D.

This paper continues the illustrations begun in Part I which described how Milton H. Erickson's utilization approach to hypnotic suggestion can facilitate the experience of profound amnesias and visual hallucinations in everyday family life. The source of Erickson's work and thinking in this area is then traced to his earliest academic training and research in the classical association theory of turn-of-the-century psychology. An updating of Erickson's utilization approach from this base in classical association theory to modern state–dependent memory and learning theory is currently establishing a new context for conceptualizing the foundations of suggestion and mind-body healing via therapeutic hypnosis.

Introduction

In a previous paper (Erickson, 1985), three principles that are characteristic of Milton H. Erickson's utilization approach to hypnotic suggestion were illustrated: 1) the hypnotic state is an experience that belongs to

Address reprint requests to: Ernest L. Rossi, Ph.D., 11980 San Vicente Blvd., Los Angeles, CA 90049.

the subject; 2) deep trance experience involves a utilization of the subject's memories of well-motivated life experiences ("experiential learnings"); and 3) mental mechanisms and sets are evoked and utilized to facilitate hypnotic suggestion. These principles led me to summarize the major historical paradigms of psychotherapy aphoristically as follows: Sigmund Freud was a genius of *analysis;* Carl Jung was a genius of *synthesis;* and Milton Erickson was a genius of *utilization.*

In this paper I present a recounting of one of Erickson's favorite stories of how he facilitated the experience of a visual hallucination in his wife, Betty. No elaborate, formal hypnotic induction was required. Rather, it was accomplished by utilizing the events of everyday life in the Erickson household.

Indirect Trance Induction Via Memories of Autohypnosis

In the living room of his home, Erickson wanted to give a demonstration of hypnosis to a visiting professional. He called his wife Betty to join them from the kitchen and asked her to describe the process of autohypnosis to the visitor. Betty Erickson is a well-rehearsed subject in autohypnosis. Erickson knew that as she recounted the process of going into autohypnosis, she would automatically put herself into a trance by association. He let her take all the time she wanted.

Utilization of a Favorite Memory to Facilitate a Positive Hallucination

When Betty was in trance, Erickson turned to the door and said, "Why, hello, Dr. M-1!" [The reason for the designation of "M-1" will become clear later.] Dr. M-1 was Betty's favorite professor at the university where she had gotten her degree. She had not seen him for 15 years.* She looked up in that automatic manner characteristic of subjects in a somnambulistic trance. Erickson asked her who was in the room. She replied that she, Erickson, and Dr. M-1 were present. The visitor was not included. Erickson persisted by asking, "Anyone else?", to which Betty replied, "No." She spoke with the hallucinated figure of Dr. M-1 for a few moments. She was in a hypnotic trance with eyes wide open. The visitor was standing in front of her, yet she did not see him. She had a negative hallucination for the visitor standing in front of her and a positive hallucination for the professor she had not seen for 15 years.

Erickson continued his description of the event as follows: "I had her

---

*After reading this paper, Betty Erickson noted that during this 15-year period, occasional letters, Christmas cards, and messages were exchanged with Dr. M-1 and his wife.

awaken. I immediately engaged her in a moment of social conversation and then let her return to the kitchen. After a period of five minutes I had the visitor go into the kitchen and ask Betty if she had been in a trance today. She replied, somewhat surprised, that she had not—did her husband want her to? She had a spontaneous amnesia for the entire incident."

The Dynamics of Hypnotic Amnesia

Why did Betty have an amnesia for her hypnotic experience?

1. Trance was indirectly induced by asking her to describe her subjective experiences of going into autohypnotic trances. As she did so, Betty went into a trance again without realizing it was happening. In the awake state, she had no opportunity to identify and label the situation as a trance experience. As she awakened, Erickson began a casual social conversation that immediately distracted Betty so that she had no opportunity to reflect upon her trance. Thus, possible associative bridges between trance and the awake state were prevented from being formed.

2. The trance occurred in the living room. She went back to the kitchen in the waking state. All trance associations were thus left behind in the living room. Any potential associations between trance and awake states were prevented by this relocation.

3. A period of five minutes was allowed to elapse between the end of the trance and questioning her about it.

4. Erickson had the visitor, who had *not* been a part of her trance, question her about it in the kitchen—away from the living room which held the trance associations.

These four factors tended to prevent the possibility of bridging associations being built between that particular trance and the awake state. *Indirect induction* and relocation via *place* (living room and kitchen), *time* (a five-minute hiatus), and *interpersonal* setting (questioned by a visitor who did not belong to the trance experience) prevented the formation of bridging associations and permitted an amnesia to develop. Hypnotic amnesia, then, is simply a matter of breaking or preventing the formation of associative bridges between trance and the awake state.

The Dynamics of the Negative and Positive Visual Hallucinations

1. The negative visual hallucination of the visitor occurred simply because he was Erickson's visitor and not related to Betty in any way. The visitor was not important in Betty's trance, so he was not in rapport and therefore not seen.

2. Two weeks prior to this experience, the Ericksons were visited by another professor whom Betty liked very much, whose name also began with *M* (thus we shall designate him as Dr. M-2), and who taught the same subject as Dr. M-1. On this occasion the Ericksons went to dinner with Dr. M-2 and his wife, and the Ericksons spoke about their last *visit* to Dr. M-1 which had taken place so long ago. Betty then remarked *how nice it would be to see him again.*

3. Dr. M-2's wife had remarkable mental talents. She would respond to a visitor's greeting, for example, with a number that would prove to be the exact number of letters contained in that greeting. She could immediately rearrange any spoken sentence into an anagram, and so on. In this way, an experience of *expectation* and *surprise* from Dr. M-2 and his wife was now associated in Betty's mind with her memories of Dr. M-1.*

4. The Ericksons frequently had visitors from all over the world who would casually drop in to see Milton, often without any forewarning of their arrival. Thus it was entirely possible that Dr. M-1 might someday be a visitor to their home. He would be greeted initially by the Ericksons in that very living room, and on that very spot where Betty had hallucinated him. Erickson would be sitting in his usual chair, and he would look up and greet Dr. M-1 just as he had done to initiate Betty's hallucination.

We can summarize some of the associative connections and mental sets that made Betty's hallucination of Dr. M-1 possible:

1. Dr. M-1 was a deep memory trace within Betty who was associated with much positive regard. This positive regard and her desire to *see* him again was a motivation for the positive hallucination.

2. The deep memory trace had been activated two weeks previously via the visit by Dr. M-2 and his wife to the Ericksons' home. The name and career similarities between Dr. M-1 and Dr. M-2, together with an almost identical history of Betty's personal and social relationships with them, had reactivated her memories of Dr. M-1.

3. New associations of *visit, expectation,* and *surprise* were also made to Dr. M-1 when he was recalled during dinner by the Ericksons and by Dr. M-2 and his wife.

---

*Betty Erickson notes that there were even more similarities in the history of her personal and social relationships with Drs. M-1 and M-2 than are reported in this paper. For example, she was initially in awe of both of them as brilliant men; she and Milton later became personal friends with them and their wives and knew them as "couples"; there was a similar exchange of occasional letters, Christmas cards, and so forth. Both Drs. M-1 and M-2 thus fit a number of similar mental sets in Betty's mind. The associative overlap of these many mental frameworks set the stage for the visual hallucination.

4. The immediate situation of having a *visit* from another *doctor in their home,* even though he was not related to Drs. M-1 and M-2, nor to Betty, nonetheless evoked another important associative mental set for the hallucination: *a visitor who was a doctor in Betty's home.*

5. The form of Erickson's hypnotic suggestion, "Why, hello, Dr. M-1!", was a startling greeting that implied a surprise visit from Dr. M-1. This surprise was entirely possible because the Ericksons did get such surprise visitors.

6. The suggestion was made in the exact appropriate location in the Ericksons' living room, where Betty hallucinated him.

Discussion

It is interesting at this point to contrast the dynamics of this visual hallucination with the amnesia so closely associated with it. The visual hallucination was built up of many positive associative connections. The amnesia was possible via the breaking of other associative connections. Amnesia and visual hallucination—two seemingly different hypnotic phenomena—are thus facilitated in essentially the same way: *by either summating or separating memory associations.*

It is important to recognize that Erickson thought of his work in terms of *association theory.* He has noted how his earliest research in hypnosis "was based upon a consideration of the concepts of introspection developed by E. B. Titchener, Wilhelm Wundt, W. B. Pillsbury and others," who were classical associationists (Erickson, 1964/1980, p. 4). Much of his earliest experimental research on hypnosis (see Volumes 2 and 3 of Erickson, 1980) centered around the measurement and utilization of word association processes. Erickson was a lover of words and their meanings, and of literature of all kinds. He was fond of telling the story about how he and a Russian colleague once sat down and found approximately 140 different meanings to the word *run.* Is it any wonder that one of his sons, Robert, who is a teacher, collects dictionaries as a hobby?

An early (1945) book-length illustration of how Erickson first *analyzed* and then *utilized* memories and the classical Freudian mental mechanisms to explore the psychodynamics of a young woman's swimming phobia is presented in *The February Man* (Rossi, in preparation). To update and integrate Erickson's approach with research in modern psychology, we (Erickson & Rossi, 1974/1980; Erickson, Rossi, & Rossi, 1976) initially used Fischer's concept of statebound memory and learning (Fischer, 1971a, b, c; Rossi, 1986b) to account for the association structures underlying hypnotic phenomena, trance experience, and everyday consciousness as follows:

Researchers (Fischer, 1971) have recently investigated *state-dependent learning* in a number of ways. One group of subjects memorize nonsense syllables while drunk. It is then found that they are better able to recall them on a later occasion when they are drunk than when they are sober. Recall is thus state-dependent; recall takes place better when people are in the same state they were in when exposed to the learning. Other investigators verified the same state-dependent phenomenon with amphetamine-induced excitatory states and amobarbitual-induced inhibitory states. Fischer generalizes these results into a theory of "how multiple existence became possible by living from waking state to another waking state; from one dream to the next; from LSD to LSD; from one creative, artistic, religious, or psychotic inspiration or possession to another; from trance to trance; and from reverie to reverie."

We would submit that therapeutic trance itself can be most usefully conceptualized as but one vivid example of *the fundamental nature of all phenomenological experience as "state-bound."* The apparent continuity of consciousness that exists in everyday normal awareness is in fact a precarious illusion that is only made possible by the associative connections that exist between related bits of conversation, task orientation, and so on. We have all experienced the instant amnesias that occur when we go too far on some tangent so we "lose the thread of thought" or "forget just what we were going to do." Without the bridging associative connections, consciousness would break down into a series of discrete states with as little contiguity as is apparent in our dream life. (Erickson, Rossi, & Rossi, 1976, p. 299)

Recent breakthroughs in the neurobiology of memory and learning have greatly extended the range and significance of classical association theory by updating it into state-dependent theory. It has been found (Izquierdo, 1984; McGaugh, 1983; Zornetzer, 1978) that hormones released during the stress of any important positive or negative life experience play an important role in the encoding, processing, and recall of memory and learning (Rossi, 1986b; Rossi & Ryan, 1986). These are the same hormones that Selye (1976) found to be the basis of the stress response and psychosomatic problems. These unexpected connections between memory, learning, and the stress response led me to integrate this new neurobiological research with the complementary psychosomatic work of Hans Selye and Milton Erickson. This, in turn, led to the formulation of a state-dependent memory and learning theory for reconceptualizing the foundations of mind-body healing via therapeutic hypnosis, visualization, meditation, biofeedback, and the placebo response (Rossi, 1986a, b).

Summary

1. Milton H. Erickson's utilization approach to hypnotic suggestion is illustrated with an example of how he facilitated the experience of a pro-

found amnesia and positive and negative visual hallucinations in his wife during the course of their everyday life.

2. The psychodynamics of these hypnotic phenomena were identified as the process of making and breaking associative connections and mental sets within the subject's previous life experience and memory systems. The background of Erickson's utilization approach to facilitating hypnotic phenomena in this manner was traced to his early training in the classical association theory of turn-of-the-century psychology (Wundt, Titchener, Pillsbury, and so forth).

3. An updating of Erickson's utilization approach via recent research in the neurobiology of state-dependent memory and learning is currently establishing a new context for conceptualizing the common denominator of mind-body healing via therapeutic hypnosis and a variety of other approaches.

References

Erickson, M. (1964/1980). Initial experiments investigating the nature of hypnosis. In E. Rossi (Ed.), *The collected papers of Milton H. Erickson on hypnosis. Vol. I. The nature of hypnosis and suggestion* (pp. 3-18). New York: Irvington.

Erickson, M. (1980). *The collected papers of Milton H. Erickson on hypnosis (Vol. I-IV).* New York: Irvington.

Erickson, M. (1985). Memory and hallucination, Part I: The utilization approach to hypnotic suggestion. Edited with commentaries by Ernest Rossi. *Ericksonian Monographs, 1,* 1-21.

Erickson, M., & Rossi, E. (1974/1980). Varieties of hypnotic amnesia. In E. Rossi (Ed.), *The collected papers of Milton H. Erickson on hypnosis. Vol. III. Hypnotic investigation of psychodynamic processes* (pp. 71-90). New York: Irvington.

Erickson, M., Rossi, E., & Rossi, S. (1976). *Hypnotic realities.* New York: Irvington.

Fischer, R. (1971a). Arousal-statebound recall of experience. *Diseases of the Nervous System, 32,* 373-382.

Fischer, R. (1971b). The "flashback": Arousal-statebound recall of experience. *Journal of Psychedelic Drugs, 3,* 31-39.

Fischer, R. (1971c). A cartography of ecstatic and meditative states. *Science, 174,* 897-904.

Izquierdo, I. (1984). Endogenous state-dependency: Memory depends on the relation between the neurohumoral and hormonal states present after training at the time of testing. In G. Lynch, J. McGaugh, & N. Weinberg (Eds.), *Neurobiology of learning and memory* (pp. 65-77). New York: Guilford Press.

McGaugh, J. (1983). Preserving the presence of the past: Hormonal influences on memory storage. *American Psychologist, 38*(2), 161-173.

Rossi, E. (1986a). Altered states of consciousness in everyday life: The ultradian rhythms. In B. Wolman & M. Ullman (Ed.), *Handbook of altered states of consciousness* (pp. 97-132). New York: Van Nostrand.

Rossi, E. (1986b). *The psychobiology of mind-body healing: New concepts of therapeutic hypnosis.* New York: Norton.

Rossi, E. (In preparation). *The February Man.* New York: Brunner/Mazel.

Rossi, E., & Ryan, M. (Eds.). (1986). *Mind-body communication in hypnosis. Vol. III. The seminars, lectures, and workshops of Milton H. Erickson.* New York: Irvington.

Selye, H. (1976). *The stress of life.* New York: McGraw-Hill.

Zornetzer, S. (1978). Neurotransmitter modulation and memory: A new neuro-pharmacological phrenology? In M. Lipton, A. Di Mascio, & K. Killam (Eds.), *Psychopharmacology: A generation of progress.* New York: Raven Press.

The Self and Its Survival in the Work of Milton Erickson

James R. Allen, M.D.

Utilization and transformation of self-perceptions seem to lie at the heart of Milton Erickson's work. Drawing on relatively well-known and previously published case studies, the author delineates five major groups of techniques used by Erickson to create, repair, reorganize, or transform the self-perceptions of his patients. These are: 1) the development of new self-perceptions; 2) the enhancement and extension of needed self-perceptions; 3) the interjection and transformation of an idealized other; 4) the use of dissociated processes; and 5) the use of pacing and mirroring.

The first three sets of these techniques seem to do more than reorganize or restructure old material, as Erickson himself believed he was doing. Rather, they introduce some new experience, some new memory or feeling, as will be discussed in terms of non-Ericksonian frameworks, particularly from the perspectives of child development and the Self Theory of Heinz Kohut.

Provision for the symbolic immortality of his patients' selves is also proposed as a major, if neglected, thrust in Erickson's therapy. Four provisions frequently implicit in his work are: 1) living on through one's children or through mankind, 2) living on through one's work, 3) the sense of being survived by nature, and 4) experiential transcendence, as in the "continuous present" of the trance state itself.

Address reprint requests to: James R. Allen, M.D., 2441 East 31st Street, Tulsa, OK 74105.

The author is indebted to the works of the Lanktons, Haley, Rossi, Zeig, the participants of two recent Erickson conferences in Phoenix, as well as many others who have reported and discussed these cases. Since so many authors have discussed the same cases—although from a different perspective than this paper—I have generally listed, for the sake of brevity, only one. However, I wish to express my indebtedness to them all.

Erickson once stated, "You see, in brief psychotherapy, one of the most important considerations is the body-image." Body-image, he explained, implies not only the "physical self" but the functional self and the personality within the body. Body-image involves "the way you see yourself, the way you appear in your mind's eye, the way you think about your body" (Haley, 1973b, p. 93). It is the purpose of this paper to expand on this brief reference in Haley, as well as on hints in Rossi (1980) and a major chapter on self-image thinking in *The Answer Within* (Lankton & Lankton, 1983).

Clients come to therapy in order to experience things differently, and much of Erickson's work can be seen as the rearrangement of self-perceptions. Sometimes, this was accomplished by reflecting a specific image to the client. Sometimes, it occurred through offering a relationship of unconditional acceptance. At times, Erickson mobilized the client to behave differently so that he might conceptualize himself differently. At other times, the change was facilitated through use of symbols or reframing.

To understand this variety of approaches, we need to recognize the numerous factors that exist in self-perception. We cannot visualize our body as a whole; hence, our idea of our bodies is really a conceptual composite of several body images. These images are mental representations of our physical selves, of past sensory experiences, and of observations of social actions.

Perhaps in his response, Erickson might well have added that the complement of one's representations of oneself is one's images of others (Spitz, 1957). Such images carry the memories of our interpersonal experiences and are the means through which our past experiences influence our present and future, for they affect our expectations of and our reactions to others. Thus, our body images, as Erickson used the term, have two important aspects. First, they help focus our self-concept and sense of self. Second, by mirroring both our appearances and our effects on others, they act as blueprints for behavior.

Repair, reorganization, transformation, and creation of self-perceptions seem to lie at the heart of Erickson's work. Erickson himself, however, was modest, believing that he was only *reorganizing* rather than synthesizing new psychic structures (Rossi, 1980). As he wrote,

> The induction and maintenance of a trance serves to provide a special psychological state in which the patient can reassociate and reorganize his inner psychological complexities.... It is this experience of reassociating and reorganizing his own experiential life that eventuates a cure. (Rossi, 1980, p. 461)

Erickson's students have used several frameworks to explain his work, but none have claimed to be fully adequate to the task. Currently, however, a number of other clinicians and researchers have been addressing the problems of the self-image. Some of these findings will complement the Ericksonian approach. Of most interest are findings on how various self-images unite to form a cohesive sense of self, and how a person experiences himself as a cohesive entity with both unity and continuity. Indeed, recent developments in the studies of child development, object-relations theory, and in Heinz Kohut's Self Theory have created major upheavals in some psychoanalytic circles. Let us begin to make a bridge to this growing body of literature and to highlight how hypotheses concerning the self can enrich our understanding of Erickson's work.

Integrating these theories is not easy because this area of inquiry is somewhat convulted and major authors show little agreement with one another. We do not even have generally-accepted definitions of such terms as "body-image," "self-image," "self-representation," or the "self," whether the latter be spelled with or without a capital. Perhaps, like a Buddhist, we might wisely regard this relatively unobscured darkness as a "creative void."

For practical purposes, it seems that each of the ways we record or remember ourselves mentally has autonomy, yet connects with most of the others. Each represents a person's way of feeling and knowing about his existence, and each is inseparable from the others which make up the overall constellation of the self. Each may be conscious or unconscious. In normal development, change can be experienced in any of them, while a person's overall sense of self retains a feeling of essential sameness. Finally, each self-image also contains an implicit potential for action. Thus, as one's self-images change, so do one's potential range of behaviors, a concept of major importance for the psychotherapist.

It would seem important not to reify the self as some sort of developmental acquisition. Rather, it seems better conceptualized as a process or a set of processes which increase in complexity as development proceeds over the life cycle. Gender identity, for example, becomes consolidated in the second and third year (Money & Ehrdardt, 1972; Jacklin & Maccoby, 1978; Galenson & Roiphe, 1971). The developing complexity of a sense of self in adolescence has been documented by Erik Erikson (1950), and the integration of self-experience in midlife by Jung (1939)—to say nothing of the current plethora of popular books on the stages of adult development. In discussions of integrative self-experiences in later life, Erikson (1950) wrote of "ego integrity" and "despair" for his eighth stage, and Kohut described late middle age as "critically significant in the life curve of the self" (1984, p. 241).

Let us now turn to an examination of the five groups of methods Erickson used to repair, reorganize, transform, and even create new self-perceptions.

The Development of a Needed Self-Image

The Creation of a Nonexistent Past

Although not the most common of his techniques, the introduction of a nonexistent past is certainly one of the most dramatic.

A young woman came to Erickson troubled that she might not be able to properly care for any children she might have because she had received so little emotional nurturance herself (Erickson & Rossi, 1979). She knew nothing good about childhood from her own experiences of growing up. Erickson used age regression to appear to her either just before or just after important events in her childhood, and instructed her not to remember anything consciously that occurred in these trances as far as the verbal content was concerned, but to keep the emotional values, enjoy them, and eventually share them with any children she might have.

Thus, it was possible, as the *February Man*, for him to interject into her memories a sense of being accepted and of sharing with a real person the important events in her early life, and for her to form new images of herself as a person who had been more adequately nurtured (Erickson & Rossi, 1979). This therapy would clearly seem to involve the creation of a new self-image rather than the reorganization of old material. In a similar vein, the Lanktons (Lankton & Lankton 1983, pp. 31-34) suggested that Erickson thereby helped her build a self-image with associated feelings of confidence and which included a variety of scenarios related to rearing children.

Pseudo-Orientation in Time

Erickson described a number of cases in which he allowed the patient, while in a trance state, to fantasize solutions to problems (Erickson, 1954). In these examples, he placed emphasis on fantasies about the future, but he made an effort to keep these fantasies unconscious. As he stated:

Each patient's unconscious was provided with a wealth of formulated ideas unknown to his conscious mind. Then, in response to the innate needs and desires of the total personality, the unconscious could utilize these ideas by translating them into realities of daily life as spontaneous responsive behavior in opportune situation. (Erickson, 1954, pp. 261-283)

The Enhancement of New Self-Perception

The Expansion of Self-Images Through the Use of "Accidental"
Life Experiences

The use of behavioral tasks was a significant feature of Erickson's work. All these tasks seem to involve expansion of the patient's self-images. Frequently, they also involved the development of relationships with others. As many have noted, Erickson was an expert in utilizing community resources and in establishing social networks. Developmentally, it is worth noting, the emergence of the self seems to occur as part of the development of awareness of others, as pointed out by Cooley (1912) and Mead (1934).

Simple techniques

At times, Erickson seems to have set a series of straightforward objectives, each building on the ones before it, to meet a more complex goal. Sometimes, this goal was nothing less than the transformation of a personality and took years to accomplish.

The case of Harold. A migratory laborer with homosexual leaning named Harold presented himself to Erickson as follows, "Mister, I'm a moron, a dumb moron. I can work, I don't want nothing but to be happy instead of scared to death and crying and wanting to kill myself (Haley, 1973b, p. 120).

Erickson accepted his view, as he typically accepted his patients' views in the beginning, but emphasized that Harold would "have to accept all the happiness that was rightfully his, no matter how small or how large a portion it was" (p. 123), defining the situation in such a way that Harold could accept or reject his suggestions in accordance with his needs. In this way, Erickson believed that nothing alien to the personality would result, and yet the potential for significant change would still be present. Two years later, Harold was attending college and beginning heterosexual relationships.

In his treatment of Harold, Erickson seems to have had two major interrelated goals: enhancement of Harold's ability to be social, and improvement in his social status. First, finding a positive aspect of Harold's life—his ability to do hard work—Erickson dignified it by quoting the biblical statement that there was an important function for the poor ("The poor are always with us"); then, emphasized the good worker as needed for a feeling of well-being, and a good diet, and later, of more comfortable living arrangements and good clothing.

In developing Harold's ability to engage in normal courtship activities, Erickson arranged for him to make friends first with a married couple, next with a man, then with an elderly woman from whom he could learn to play the piano but to whose welfare he could also contribute (yardwork). Finally, Erickson had him learn to dance. After some trance sessions in which Harold was instructed to render to a "limited number" of poor souls "the help they wanted in a detached impersonal way," Harold went to a public dance and "spontaneously" asked several wallflowers to dance—and experienced a sense of accomplishment.

By the time Harold was preparing to begin normal heterosexual activities, Erickson had done much to create an atmosphere where this could occur "spontaneously." By then, Harold was living in a respectable apartment, dressing properly, and working at a good job. He had studied music and cooking, had had good experiences in social relationships, and had developed a curiosity about "what kind of a critter" a woman is.

Thus, we can see that Erickson had carefully built up the skills Harold would eventually need. He also had helped Harold develop a range of social bonds—friendships, work, and nurturance. It is typical of his approach, as Haley (1973b) pointed out, that he achieved this by giving vague directions at first, then arranging particular social contacts and letting the interaction develop spontaneously. Thus, the patient had a feeling that the accomplishment was his alone, and, perhaps more importantly, he had accomplished it in his own unique way, so that "nothing alien to the personality results."

The self can be conceptualized as one's social roles, and Erickson had carefully helped Harold develop several new, but necessary ones. Harold had developed a whole new view of himself and of what he was capable.

The case of the restaurateur.   In the case of a couple who quarreled constantly about the management of their restaurant (Haley, 1973b, p. 226)—the wife insisted that her husband manage it, but he insisted that she never let him do so—Erickson suggested that she see to it that he arrive at the restaurant one half-hour before she did.

Erickson still let her be in charge, but it was in a way that would allow her attention to turn toward taking care of their home, which she actually preferred to do. Thus, he set in motion a positive feedback mechanism: If she could be a half-hour late, she could just as easily be one hour late. As Erickson commented to colleagues, the husband would not be able to understand how he had been inviting her into the restaurant, but he could understand that he could be in charge of the place and could be comfortable being in charge.

There appear to be two main varieties of this use of life experiences in Erickson's work:

Expansion. At times, Erickson helped the patient develop new self-images around already existent core areas of the self. The two cases cited above are examples of this. Here is an example of a less complex one.

Finding that a depressed, lonely, and isolated woman had a few African Violet plants, Erickson insisted that she buy 200 pots and give African Violets for every anniversary, birthday, and church bazaar. Thus, she was transformed from a lonely, old woman into the *African Violet Queen* of her area (Zeig, 1980).

In this example, Erickson took advantage of the one kind of activity she performed—nurturance—and expanded it so that she developed "spontaneous" friendships and work bonds.

Substitution. When consulted by a woman bereft by the death of her daughter, Erickson suggested she plant a eucalyptus tree (a fast growing tree) and name it Cynthia after her daughter (Zeig, 1980). He promised to return in one year to sit with her in Cynthia's shade. In this example, the tree was substituted for the daughter—a tree which she could nurture and which would later provide nurturance and protection for her.

Members of the Chicago school of sociology and social psychology have argued that the self is not something disembodied, but emerges out of the interactions between an individual and those about him. These relationships have a structure provided by the individual's social roles. The relationship between social roles and psychopathology is circular. Disturbances in social role can lead to psychopathology just as psychopathology can lead to impairment of social role-performance. Traditional psychiatric thinking—with the notable exception of Harry Stack Sullivan (1953) and his followers—has tended to emphasize only the latter.

American social scientists have emphasized the benefits of social ties and have generally suggested that individuals establish social ties in order to strengthen personality. In contrast to this tradition of Cooley (1912), Mead (1934), Dewey (1922), Homans (1950), Sullivan (1953), Cobb (1976), and Caplan (1974), and European writers, such as LeBon (1896) and Simmel (1950), have tended to stress the negative potentials of these networks. It is clear that Erickson belongs to the first group.

In many of his case reports, Erickson's descriptions end with the couple getting married and having several children. Commentators have sometimes attributed this apparent simplicity to the man's rural upbringing. It is not coincidental, however, that in their national survey, Campbell, Converge, and Rogers (1976) found that general life satisfaction correlated most strongly with family and marriage, then with satisfaction in occupation and friendships.

There appear to be at least three ways in which social ties are supportive of a sense of well-being (House, 1980). Informational support is the provision of advice and knowledge. Functional support is tangible help. Emotional support is an emotional alliance. At least one kind of emotional support consists of the assurance of an alliance with a figure of unquestionable strength (Burnand, 1965). Erickson was, of course, the quintessence of such a figure.

More complex techniques

In a famous case report (Erickson, 1955), Erickson tells of treating a woman who was set on killing herself. She told him she was unlikeable and did not interact with the men she was attracted to, although there were a number in her office. He suggested that she ought to have at least one good memory before she killed herself, and urged her to play a prank. Taking advantage of a gap between her teeth, he instructed her to go to the water cooler at her office, take a mouthful of water and, when a young man approached, to squirt him. She did. The young man chased her and kissed her—initiating a series of events which eventually led to her marriage and relief from her depression.

De Shazer (1982) has drawn attention to how Erickson sometimes reframed one aspect of a patient's complaint from an involuntary symptom to a useful and deliberate part of his or her life. Such reframing changes the meaning of the patient's situation and leads to behavior change.

Erickson made two major changes in this woman's self-image. She could no longer see herself as ugly and disfigured since the gap between her teeth helped her reach her goal. The interaction with the young man took its course, for they "spontaneously" got married, obviously creating quite a different picture than her initial image of herself as unlikeable and as someone who did not interact with men. De Shazer (1982) described five additional examples of this pattern: two cases of hysterical paralysis, a woman with gastric ulcers, an adolescent with a big tooth, and a 16-year-old thumb sucker.

The Updating of an Age-Inappropriate Self-Image

More than most therapists, Erickson seems to have kept the life cycle in mind as he created his interventions. Whatever stage of life a person is in, the transition to the next stage is crucial both for him and for his family. Haley even used this framework as the basis for one of his books on Erickson, *Uncommon Therapy* (1973b).

From a young woman who vomited when the man she long had loved leaned over to kiss her, Erickson learned that the girl's mother, just before dying, had taught her that sex was nasty and disgusting (Haley, 1973b). At first, he adopted a point of view identical to that of her mother. Later, while she was in a trance, he added, "Had your mother lived longer, she would have talked to you many more times to give you advice. But because she died when you were only thirteen, she could not complete that task and you had to complete it without help" (p. 79). When, at the end of three sessions, she seemed to have accepted this idea in both trance and waking states, Erickson had her forget all three sessions completely but instructed her to find truths and applications understandable only to her as he presented a systematic review of sexual development.

Thus, she developed "insight" gradually and in a progressive fashion. More importantly, her concept of herself and of what was acceptable sexual behavior for her gradually became more age-appropriate. In this example, her self-concept was updated. However, Erickson may also have been interjected as an "idealized other."

The Interjection and Transformation of an Idealized Other

"And my voice will go with you" is a phrase that Rosen transformed into the title of his book on Erickson (Rosen, 1982). With these words, Erickson suggests to a patient that his voice will go with her, will become the voice of her parents, then her own, then the sound of the wind and the rain.

According to Rosen, this was a phrase Erickson frequently used. While this might be interpreted as a confusion technique, it can also be understood in a very different way. Kohut (1971, 1977) theorized that the self has three basic poles: one arising from a primitive grandiose self, one from an idealized other, and a third, a pole of talents and skills, lying between them. Those with a damaged pole of ambitions attempt, he believed, to elicit approving and confirming responses ("mirror transference"). Those with a damaged pole of ideals search for people to idealize ("idealizing transference"). Those with damage in the area of skills and talents seek the reassurance of those who are essentially like themselves ("twinship transference"). In this instance, Erickson seems to have interjected himself as an idealized other, and then set in motion some kind of transformation of the introject. However, because of the ambiguity of his instructions, the patient could also respond by experiencing Erickson as being silently present but in essence like himself. Thus, the pole of ambitions, the pole of ideals, and the intermediate pole of skills and talents could be maintained.

Silverman (1978) has summarized a large number of research studies demonstrating that the activation of unconscious fantasies of union with the mother can have an ameliorative effect on psychopathology of all kinds. Expressed in a verbal form, the fantasy is best conveyed in the words, *Mommy and I are one.* Such a fantasy can be understood as related to the symbiotic phase of development so extensively described by Mahler and her colleagues (Mahler, Pine, & Bergman, 1975). Drawing on the work of Kohut, Silverman commented, "If the need is restitutive, a result of early developmental failure, one can anticipate the possibility of structural changes and symptom amelioration" (Silverman, 1978, p. 586). Thus, in the apparently simple phrase "And my voice will go with you," Erickson may well have set in motion primitive healing fantasies of merger.

The Elaboration of New Self-Images and the
Enhancement and Extension of Neglected Ones
Through Dissociated Processes

A variety of techniques that have come to be recognized as "Ericksonian" can be used to help a patient elaborate new self-images or to revise or extend older ones. For example, an obese, unkempt, "obnoxiously dirty" woman who despaired of ever getting a date was presented with a mirror, weight chart, and scales (Haley, 1973b, p. 93). For three hours, Erickson led her through a straightforward and complete critique of her appearance. He handed her a washcloth and instructed her to wash one side of her neck, then to contrast it to the other side. At the next session—to which she came well-groomed—she was told she never would be able to forget something which she apparently had failed to notice but which was apparent to everyone else. As she left, he said, "You are never going to be able to forget that you have a pretty patch of fur between your legs. Now go home, undress, get in the nude, stand in front of a mirror, and you will see the three beautiful badges of womanhood. They are with you always wherever you go, and you cannot forget them ever again." In her shock, she may not have been able consciously to ward off what he said. It is typical of Erickson that he sought to expand the patient's world and not just educate her out of her defects.

When a person fails to deal with a conflict, a part of his self-experience may be made inaccessible to the remainder of the experienced self. If some of these unacceptable self-images become accessible to awareness, he may not be able to blend them with other self-images without a loss of sense of cohesion. This problem can be handled therapeutically through the use of reframing, a technique well-described elsewhere (Lankton & Lankton, 1980; Gordon & Meyers-Anderson, 1981; Erickson, Rossi, & Rossi, 1976).

Erickson's work with patients in trance is the model par excellence of work at the level of dissociated processes. Here his description of work as the reorganization and reassociation of inner psychological complexities seems most accurate.

The Use of Pacing to Affirm Self-Perceptions

Now let us turn to an interpersonal aspect of technique which applies to enhancing the self. The value of accepting and utilizing a client's reality was stressed by Erickson and is the major theme of Erickson and Rossi's *Hypnotherapy* (1979). Accepting means assuming and communicating to the patient that what he is doing is exactly right. Bandler and Grinder (1975) discussed these principles in the more process-oriented terms of *pacing* and *leading*. Pacing is feeding back to the patient his own experience: It adds nothing new. Gilligan (1984) has suggested that when the therapist synchronizes with patterns that the patient consciously or unconsciously identifies as patterns unique to himself, the patient feels safe and can let go and enter a trance.

Through repetitious behaviors we maintain our identity and a particular state of consciousness. Through pacing, the therapist takes the patient's intrapsychic processes into the interpersonal sphere. The patient is thus freed to explore the autonomous and generative processes of his or her unconscious. Trance, according to Gilligan (1984), somehow unbinds the underlying constraints that maintain the organizational unit of the self. A new organizational unit can then emerge.

Careful pacing also validates a person's self-perceptions, either because the therapist mirrors him much as a mother mirrors her infant, or because it allows the patient to grasp his inner life more or less accurately—a response which somehow reactivates thwarted developmental needs of the self.

One current focus in infant research which would seem important in understanding the role of pacing is the examination of behavioral "synchrony." Behavioral synchrony refers to the predisposition of infants and parents to mesh their behavior in timed, mutual interchanges, and has been examined from the point of view of microanalysis of arousal and looking (Stern, 1977; Brazelton and Als, 1979), of voice and movement (Condon and Sandler, 1974), and of behavioral state (Sandler, 1975).

A number of infant observers such as Mahler and Fauer (1968), Kohut

(1971), and the Papouseks (1979) have pointed out the importance of such parental mirroring for self-development. Indeed, parental mirroring may offer the infant opportunities for controlling parental behavior. Even the words mothers create from infant vocalization, such as "ba-ba" which later becomes "baby," usually relate to the self. This interpersonal process, then, of pacing seems integral both to normal development of the child's self and to the therapeutic repair of the client's sense of self.

The Survival of the Self

While it is well known that Erickson twice suffered from devastating bouts with polio, twice coming close to death, there has been little attention given to the therapeutic importance of Erickson as a survivor: He came into contact with death, but remained alive. He explained what he learned from these experiences and from watching others, while unable to move himself. It is not unimportant to note the human tendency to expect those who go through such an encounter with death to return with something special to teach us, perhaps even the secret of how to survive.

From his studies of death and destruction, Lifton (1984, pp. 31-34) delineated five general modes of seeking immortality for the self. These are: living through one's children or through mankind, living through one's works, the sense of being survived by nature, experiential transcendence, and a belief in life after death. The first three of these modes are implicit in Erickson's work, and many people experience the trance state itself as a transcendency.

We live on, in and through our children, imagining some endless succession of biological extension. This mode of symbolic immortality perhaps reached its most classical expression in traditional China with its emphasis on family life. In Confucian ethics, for example, the worst of unfilial acts was not to have children. However, symbolic immortality is not exclusively biological, for it also expresses itself in attachment to one's group, one's people, and one's nation. Ultimately, we can catch at least a glimmering of immortality in living through and in mankind. A second mode of symbolic immortality is achieved through one's works and one's influence.

The sense of being survived by or becoming part of nature is a third approach. This was a major aspect of the European Romantic movement. Gandhi had his ashes scattered in all states of India and his bones cast into the waters where the Ganges and Jumma rivers are believed to be joined by a third celestial river. The ashes of Erickson were scattered on Squaw Peak, a mountain peak near his home in Arizona.

In experiential transcendence, time and death disappear. This can occur in a number of contexts, including the trance state. It includes a feeling of what Eliade (1959) termed the "continuous present," a present which is perceived both as here and now, inseparable from both the past and the future.

These means of achieving symbolic immortality, of survival of the self, are frequently to be found in Erickson's psychotherapy. Whether we look at the case of Harold, the "African Violet Queen," or Cynthia, we find he not only created, repaired, reorganized, or extended the self-perceptions of his clients, he also opened for them a means for symbolic survival.

Summary

With the exceptions of the use of dissociated processes and the use of pacing and mirroring, the techniques described in this paper seem to do more than reorganize or restructure old material, as Erickson himself believed. Rather, they introduce some new experience, some new memory or feeling, and seem to create new self-representation. The end result of these procedures is a new and updated image of the self. This also fits with Erickson's teaching:

> Patients have problems because their unconscious programming has too severely limited their capacities. The solution is to help them break through the limitations of their conscious attitudes to free their unconsciousness potential for problem solving. (Erickson, Rossi, & Rossi, 1976, p. 18)

These approaches also directly change the patient's conscious attitudes toward himself. Pseudo-orientation in time is an especially interesting technique for it combines both the client's unconscious reorganization and inner synthesis in the creative solution of problems, and his subsequent conscious awareness of successful new behaviors. Finally, Erickson seems frequently to have provided his clients with ways to achieve symbolic immortality.

References

Amsterdam, B. K. (1972). Mirror self-image reaction before age two. *Developmental Psychology, 5:*297-305.

Bandler, R., & Grinder, J. (1975). *Patterns of hypnotic techniques of Milton H. Erickson, M.D.* Vol. 1. Cupertino, CA: Meta Publications.

Bradburn, N., & Caploritz, D. (1965). *Reports on happiness.* Hawthorn, N.Y.: Aldine.

Brazelton, T. B., & Als, H. (1979). Four stages in the development of mother-infant interaction. *Psychoanalytic Study of the Child, 34*:349-369.

Burnand, G. (1965). The nature of emotional support. *British Journal of Psychiatry,* p. 1151.

Campbell, A., Converge, P., & Rogers, E. (1976). *The quality of American life.* New York: Russell Sage Foundation.

Caplan, G. (1974). *Support systems and community mental health.* New York: Behavioral Publications.

Cassirer, E. (1953). *The philosophy of symbolic forms, Three Volumes.* New Haven: Yale University Press.

Clarke, A.M., & Clarke, A.B.D. (1976). *Early experience.* New York: Free Press.

Cobb, S. (1976). Social support as a moderator of life stress. *Psychosomatic Medicine, 38*(5): 300–314.

Condon, W.S., & Sandler, L.W. (1974). Synchrony demonstrated between movements of the neonate and adult speech. *Child Development, 45*: 456-462.

Cooley, C.H. (1909). *Social organization.* New York: Scribner.

Cooley, C. H. (1912). *Human nature and the social order.* New York: Scribner.

De Shazer, S. (1982). *Patterns of brief family therapy.* New York: Guilford Press.

Dewey, J. (1922). *Human nature.* New York: Holt, Rinehart & Winston.

Eliade, M. (1959). *Cosmos and history: The myth of the eternal return.* New York: Torchbooks.

Erickson, M. H. (1952). *Experimental hypnosis.* New York: Macmillan. Reprinted in E. L. Rossi (Ed.) (1980). *The collected papers of Milton H. Erickson, Vol. I.* New York: Irvington.

Erickson, M. H. (1954). Pseudo-orientation in time as a hypnotherapeutic procedure. *Journal of Clinical and Experimental Hypnosis, 2*: 261-283.

Erickson, M. H. (1955). The hypnotherapy of psychosomatic dental problems. *Journal of American Society of Psychosomatic Dentistry and Medicine, 1*:6-10.

Erickson, M. H. (1980). Basic psychological problems in hypnotic research. In E. L. Rossi (Ed.), *The collected papers of Milton H. Erickson.* Vol. II. New York: Irvington.

Erickson, M. H., Rossi, E.L., & Rossi, S. I. (1976). *Hypnotic realities: The clinical hypnosis and forms of indirect suggestions.* New York: Irvington.

Erickson, M. H. & Rossi, E. (1979). *Hypnotherapy: An exploratory case book,* (Chapter 10). New York: Irvington.

Erikson, E., (1950). *Childhood and society.* New York: W.W. Norton.

Galenson, E., & Roiphe, H. (1971). The impact of early sexual discovery on mood, defensive organization, and symbolization. *Psychoanalytic Study of the Child, 26*: 195-216.

Gilligan, S. (1984). Generative autonomy: Principles for Ericksonian hypnotherapy. In J. Zeig (Ed.), *Ericksonian psychotherapy vol. 1: Structures.* New York: Brunner/Mazel.

Gilligan, S. (1985). Generative autonomy: Principles from Ericksonian hynotherapy. In J. Zeig (Ed.), *Ericksonian psychotherapy, Vol. 1, Structures* (pp. 102-105). New York: Brunner/Mazel.

Gordon, D., & Meyers-Anderson, M. (1981). *Phoenix: Therapeutic patterns of Milton H. Erickson.* Cupertino, CA: Meta Publications.

Haley, J. (Ed.). (1973a). *Advanced techniques of hypnosis and therapy.* New York: Grune and Stratton.

Haley, J. (1973b). *Uncommon therapy.* New York: W.W. Norton.

Homans, G. (1950). *The human group.* New York: Harcourt Brace Jovanovich.

House, J.S. (1980). *Work, stress and social support.* Reading, MA: Addison-Wesley.

Jacklin, C. V., & Maccoby, E. E. (1978). Social behavior at thirty-three months in same sex and mixed-set dyad. *Child Development, 49*:557-569.

Jung, C.G. (1939). *Integration of the personality.* New York: Farrar and Rinehart.

Kagan, J. (1981). *The second year.* Cambridge: Harvard University Press.

Keeney, B.L. (1983). *Aesthetics of change.* New York: Guilford.

Klerman, G., Weissman, M. M., Rounsaville, B. J., & Cherrow, E. S. (1984). *Interpersonal psychotherapy of depression.* New York: Basic Books.

Kohut, H. (1971). *The analysis of the self.* New York: International Universities Press.

Kohut, H. (1977). *The restoration of the self.* New York: International Universities Press.

Kohut, H. (1984). *How does psychoanalysis cure?* Chicago: University of Chicago Press.

Lankton, S., & Lankton, C. (1980). *Practical magic.* Cupertino, CA: Meta Publications.

Lankton, S., & Lankton, C. (1983). *The answer within.* New York: Brunner/Mazel.

LeBon, G. (1896). *The crowd.* New York: Macmillan.

Lewis, M., & Brooks-Gunn, J. (1979). *Social cognition and the acquisition of self.* New York: Plenum.

Lichtenberg, J. (1975). The Development of the Sense of Self. *Journal of the American Psychoanalysis Association, 23.* New York.

Lifton, R.J. (1984). *The life of the self.* New York: Basic Books.

Mahler, M., Pine, F., & Bergman, A. (1975). *The psychological birth of the human infant.* New York: Basic Books.

Mahler, M.S., & Furer, M. (1968). *On human symbiosis and the vicissitudes of individuation.* New York: International Universities Press.

Mead, G.H. (1934). *Mind, self and society.* Chicago: University of Chicago Press.

Money, J., & Ehrhardt, A. (1972). *Man, woman, boy and girl.* Baltimore: Johns Hopkins University Press.

Papousek, H., & Papousek, M. (1979). Early ontogeny in human social interaction. In M. Von Cronach et al. (Eds.), *Human ethnology* (pp. 456-489). Cambridge: Cambridge University Press.

Ritterman, M. (1985). Symptoms, social justice and personal freedom. *Journal of Strategic and Systemic Therapies.* Vol. 4, No. 2, September.

Rosen, S. (1982). *And my voice will go with you.* New York: W. W. Norton.

Rossi, E. (Ed.) (1980). *The collected papers of Milton Erickson,* Vol. 4. New York: Irvington.

Sackett, G., Sameroff, A.J., Cairns, R.B., & Suomi, S.J. (1981). Continuity in behavioral development. In K. Immelmann, G. Barlow, L. Petrinovich, & N. Main (Eds.), *Behavioral development* (pp. 23-57). Cambridge: Cambridge University Press.

Sameroff, A.J., & Chandler, M. (1976). Reproductive risk and the continuum of caretaking casualty. In F. D. Horwitz, (Ed.), *Review of the child development research* (4: 187-244). Chicago: University of Chicago Press.

Sandler, L. W. (1975).   Infant and caretaking environment. In E. J. Anthony (Ed.),
    Explorations in child psychiatry (pp. 129-166). New York: Plenum.
Sandler, J., & Rosenblatt, B. (1962).   The concept of the representational world.
    *Psychoanalytic Study of the Child, 17:*128-146.
Schulman, H.A., & Raplowitz, C. (1977).   Mirror image response during the first
    two years of life. *Developmental Psychology, 10:*133-144.
Silverman, L.H. (1978).   Unconscious symbiotic fantasy. An ubiquitous
    therapeutic agent. *International Journal of Psychoanalytic Psychotherapy, 7:*
    586-593.
Simmel, G. (1950). In K.H. Wolff (Ed.), *The sociology of George Simmel.* New York:
    Free Press.
Spitz, R.A. (1957).   *No and yes.* New York: International Universities Press.
Stern, D.N. (1977).   *The first relationship.* Cambridge: Harvard University Press.
Sullivan, H.S. (1953). In H.S. Perry (Ed.), *The interpersonal theory of psychiatry.* New
    York: W.W. Norton.
Zeig, J. (1980).   *A teaching seminar with Milton Erickson.* New York: Brunner/
    Mazel.

The Scramble Technique

Stephen R. Lankton, M.S.W.

The Scramble Technique is a method of utilizing a client's natural abilities to inhibit the occurrence of a symptom and replace it with necessary emotional or experiential resources. Through a series of six distinguishable phases, the stages of the symptom are identified, rehearsed in sequence, rehearsed in random (scrambled), and then replaced with a previously retrieved resource. The author's method of conducting this technique is presented with explanation and case transcript. This technique belongs within the framework of a total psychotherapy or family treatment program but is provided here in an isolated context that resulted in the successful treatment of a client experiencing anxiety-related asthma attacks. In this isolated context the phases of the technique are easily highlighted. A discussion of the proper circumstances for the use of this technique is provided.

The Scramble Technique as Brief Intervention

Traditional approaches to therapy have considered the identified patient (IP) as the problem and tend to classify clients and, therefore, design treatment on the basis of diagnostic categories. In the Ericksonian model of family therapy, psychotherapy, and hypnotherapy, the symptom is most often treated via indirect techniques that focus on evoking inner resources and abilities rather than on removing the symptom (Erickson & Rossi, 1979). I prefer to approach the identified patient (IP) as a unique individual and assess the family of the IP as a unique family. I avoid working in the role that is thrust upon me by the family. I avoid the role of taking the symptom from the IP. Often I work to help each family member gain the inner resources needed to move the entire family successfully through his or her current developmental stage. Most often this means that direct

Address reprint requests to: Stephen R. Lankton, M.S.W., P.O. Box 958, Gulf Breeze, FL 32561.

attention to symptom removal is not foremost in my plans. I have described such incidents of circuitous intervention in other works (Lankton & Lankton, 1983; Lankton, 1985).

Occasionally, however, I work directly with the presenting symptom to reduce or remove it 1) when it appears to function independently of family organization and learned roles (Lankton & Lankton, 1986; Minuchin, 1974; Madanes, 1984) or 2) when it appears that the family members are not amenable to therapy (Lankton & Lankton, 1983, pp. 291-311; Erickson & Rosen, 1980; Erickson, 1980b). Therapy involving primarily symptom-directed interventions is also the best choice 3) when the symptom has been recently learned in response to trauma (Lankton & Lankton, 1983, pp. 280-291, or 4) when the previous developmental situation that gave rise to the symptom has changed and the symptom has taken on a life of its own (Lankton & Lankton, 1983, pp. 258-291).

In situations involving a compromise of our principles, certain goals and values must be surrendered. If the client-system refuses therapy, we must choose between two unpleasant arrangements and determine which is the lesser of two evils: leave the family with no change at all, or make an attempt (although possibly futile) to remove or reduce the symptom. Usually we choose the latter. In so doing, we suspect and hope that the family will become more willing to seek therapy at a later date due to our limited success with the presenting symptom.

The Scramble Technique consists of six phases during which 1) resources are retrieved; 2) the high and low parameters of the anxiety reaction are identified; 3) the intervening stages of the anxiety reaction are identified; 4) the entire sequence is rehearsed in sequential order; 5) the entire sequence is rehearsed in random order (it is "scrambled"); and 6) the symptom is replaced by the previously retrieved resource. It is important to mention that although the Scramble Technique deals directly with the symptom, it does not necessarily take place as an intervention isolated from more comprehensive treatment.

In the following case, the Scramble intervention appears as an isolated intervention in a single-session, symptom-focused treatment. Because of this isolation, the technique is more clearly illustrated here than it might be in another context within a more comprehensive therapy. This more comprehensive therapy would usually include multiple-embedded metaphors, various assignments, and other strategic interventions designed to retrieve resources, build new roles, and foster greater interpersonal adjustment. Within that framework, the Scramble Technique can facilitate a therapeutic confusion about symptom sequence that helps the person "unlearn" the mechanics of a symptom that is no longer interpersonally necessary. The Scramble Technique is a systematic and teachable method of treating symptoms with the Confusion Technique (Erickson, 1980a).

Steps of the Scramble Technique

Retrieve Inner Resources

The first phase in the scramble is the retrieval of inner resources that can be used by the person to replace the anxiety when the scramble is completed. Usually, a pleasant feeling from a past experience is elicited to replace the symptomatic anxiety. In some instances, the criterion of pleasant is not the most therapeutically efficient or desirable to the client; a feeling-related experience of another and a more utilitarian nature (such as determination, effectiveness, competence, etc.) is then elicited to provide the necessary coping skills.

My case illustration involves a 36-year-old married man with two children, four and six years old. He would suffer from the sudden onset of asthma attacks whenever he was asked to perform. In other words, he had anxiety attacks in the form of asthmatic reactions. He is a very control-and leadership-oriented man who had been successful and locally admired and respected for his work as a family therapist. His need to be a leader is intimately tied to his self-esteem and he had difficulty asking for help himself. Both at home and on the job, he took the role of friendly leader and was thought to be both fair and firm with his family. He was not well-suited for taking the role of a client seeking help and for that reason alone he was disinclined to be a good therapy candidate. Neither was he willing to involve the rest of the family in what he considered a behavior he learned in childhood.

Ironically, at this point in his life he is not in situations where he is called upon to perform any tasks that he cannot do well. The anxiety he experienced was out of proportion to real demands. It was, to him, as if he was still performing under perfectionistic demands and without sufficient support or training. As he did not consciously place such expectations on himself, it seemed as if he had learned an automatic habit that was often triggered below the level of awareness and had diverse physiological components. Therefore, I chose to take this client as an individual and address only the symptom. In making this choice, I lost the opportunity to help elicit and guide this client's development and I must trust that he is resourceful enough to change, fittingly, the other aspects of his family communication and relations, his social role, self-image, and so forth. However, this client gave every appearance of a resourceful and capable man.

The first set of resources I wanted him to retrieve were the feelings of success and of a job well done which were already well-established in the client. The following metaphorical segment was used to help evoke these feelings after the induction of trance.

I wonder about your ability to succeed in having levitation of the hand off of the lap. And the index finger moving across the corduroy is very convenient for a conscious mind, because the stripes in the corduroy make it possible to accurately graph the gradual movement of fingers. Your thumb moved one small corduroy, and another cord, and the index finger moved half a cord. And if you grew up on a farm, you'd be thinking you had done a lot of work, already moving two-and-a-half cords! You felt like you had chopped wood all day. Whether or not you levitate that hand, you can recall experiences, even though you never lived on a farm, feeling a job well done.

As a teenager I used to try to avoid mowing the lawn many times. We had a large area of grass—the front yard, back yard, side yard. And my father, out of a streak of diabolical parenting, owned two apartments with yards front and back. And he just knew I'd be glad to mow all the grass. And to make matters worse, my mother decided not to put in a garden one year but grew grass where the garden had been. I had sort of a city full of grass to mow! And so it became a constant job.

The best resolution to the entire matter was to set my mind to the task of mowing the yard. Sometimes I'd try to get ahead of it and save my sanity by beginning on a Thursday evening; and on a Friday evening I would mow another apartment. Then, on Saturday morning I could mow the garden, and front and back and side yard, and be done with it. I always had a great feeling of satisfaction. I'd lay down in the grass on a Saturday afternoon, and my dog would come rolling and jumping on it with me, just lying there looking up at the clouds. It was the satisfaction of a hard job well done; and that I didn't have to do any more.

Living in Michigan I could always depend on the Gods of Weather to ruin one of my weekends of mowing for me. Then, pretty soon, I'd have a yard twice as deep in grass to mow! I developed a certain discipline about beginning at a certain time during the week and finishing early on Saturdays so that I'd have the rest of the weekend to myself. And I still remember those times when I'd lie down in the freshly mowed lawn, watching the Michigan clouds form overhead, the heat on my body. And I knew that physically my work was pretty much over. I knew that my parents were going to be off my back. I felt proud.

I don't know if that is still a feeling to build upon for future reference, but I know that the conscious mind can appreciate that experience. Your conscious mind may feel the experience of thinking that the job is over and that I've done a good job. Your conscious mind might think that there is some pressure, some place. I don't know whether or not you feel the experience of the job well done, or, whether it's just an idea in the mind and your unconscious takes care of the body reaction. Usually, you raise your sternum, relax your shoulders, and walk a little taller. I know consciously you can actually have pride in yourself. Everyone must have some similar experience.

Identifying Parameters of the Anxiety Response

The second phase of this intervention, and the first phase of the actual Scramble Technique, is to have the client identify the stages of the building anxiety. The actual words or symbols the client uses to identify the stages can be created "on the spot" in the office. For the client who has not previously considered the progression of the anxiety, I suggest the following procedure.

Ask the client to label the full-blown occurrence of the anxiety as stage 5, with its weakest correlate being stage 1. Stage 1 may even reflect a state-of-being that precedes conscious recognition of anxiety. Next, ask the client to imagine or create the stages and to use the labels, "stage 1" and "stage 5." One precaution must be mentioned at this point: When stage 5 involves a violent or threatening situation, the use of dissociation is strongly recommended. The client can be asked to experience the worst stage in a dissociated state so that the actual physical symptoms are not triggered by the instruction for this phase. This type of safeguard was employed in this case, as the following transcript will illustrate.

And once these feelings of pride and success are retrieved, then there is nothing else to do in the way of chores. You are prepared to go ahead and do that job with feelings of success and pride unconsciously in the background as a foundation. And I have a different view of procrastination. Now, we've been procrastinating. And I know that your unconscious is capable of recognizing that first indicator *to you* before it reaches your conscious mind, *that there would be an onset of asthma.* I'd like you to imagine or pretend or hallucinate or remember or recall or produce the very slightest indicator, and only the very slightest indicator, that could be recognized as the beginning of the onset of the asthma you spoke of earlier. And when you're aware unconsciously, perhaps even before you are consciously aware, either give me a nod of the head or raise a finger as an indicator that we can use to efficiently communicate. Call that stage 1. Find out if you can recreate it again and raise your finger and be satisfied with your ability to recognize it as stage 1.

Now I'd like you to pretend or imagine—and you may want to dissociate yourself from the experience so that you have no discomfort in the process. I probably don't need to mention that you could float out of your body and sit beside yourself in the chair. Maybe it would be convenient to sit in the audience and observe the feet on the floor, hands on the thighs midway to the knee, your corduroys, dark belt, white shirt, short sleeves, your square shoulders, broad chest breathing from the stomach, beard down to the breast, glasses on the nose a quarter inch from the eyebrows, eyes closed: your bracelet on the right arm, ring on both hands, white gear on the head, and there he sits.

It would be easy for you to use your own knowledge of dissociation if necessary, but whether it's necessary or not, locate some experience that would be considered by your conscious mind to be a full-blown aspect of the asthma symptom you spoke about. Or perhaps some experience just so close in proximity that it would be sufficient for our purposes to be considered equivalent but at the same time free of debilitating aspects. And when you are able to pretend or recall or produce or hallucinate that experience sufficiently to recognize it again, give me the same finger raise as a signal. Allow me to call it stage 5.

Identifying Sequential Stages

Once the high and low parameters of the anxiety have been identified, the intervening stages can be identified by asking the client to locate an experience that is midway between the highest and lowest points (between stages 5 and 1) and call that point 3. The logic implicit is that this bisection results in an identifiable midpoint by all but the most resistant of clients. Continuing the same line of logic, a midpoint between 3 and 1 will yield stage 2, and similarly that point between 5 and 3 will yield stage 4. This phase of the technique can be explained to the client as follows:

Now, unfortunately, you know that I'm going to ask you to recognize the reasonableness that if there's a beginning stage and an end stage, then there must be something in the middle that you can recognize as the middle stage. So, with your very best detective work, your very best geometry, find a midpoint of the experience. With your very best mathematics, divide it in half. Find the experience halfway in between that which would symbolize and indicate to you that we have that same indication. Call it stage 3. And remember that experience.

It's unfortunate that you know I'm going to ask you to find the midpoint between stage 3 and stage 5. It would be nice if it were a surprise. A draftsman would get his compass, an engineer would get his slide rule or Apple-II, and you're going to have to use your unconscious Apple-II to find the midpoint between stage 3 and stage 5. And give me the same indication that sufficient discriminative stimulus can be notified between the midpoint and the full-blown experience. Call it stage 4.

And you might want to have a moment's pause to review what you know so far. And in these first few moments there is such a delicate memorization of subtle experiences. And before you learn another one, you might want to let your thoughts go their own direction.

Now, some place between the beginning experience that you may or may not consciously be able to detect, and the midpoint which presumably has some ability to be consciously detected, there lies a midpoint, or something close to a midpoint, or some discrimination place between 1 and 3. I would like you to decide or determine where that is, and give me the same signal again when you're satisfied with your ability to detect the midpoint between 1 and 3. Call that 2.

Rehearse the Sequence

Before Scrambling the sequence, it is important to reinforce the labels the client has established for each of its segments. This can be done easily by asking the client to give a head nod, a finger lift, or some other ideomotor signal to indicate that he or she can distinguish the particular stage when it is requested. Rehearsing the stages in their proper order (1 through 5) will help the client cultivate his or her awareness of each stage. This rehearsal should be carried out five or six times, or as many times as is necessary to ensure that each stage is easily distinguishable by the client.

> Now, let's review, giving me your signal again so that I know how fast the stages can be perceived, beginning with stage 1. When you have that, give me the signal. Now go to stage 2. Now, at your own speed, give me the signal there. And now go to stage 3 and give me the signal you've gotten there. And now stage 4; when you've gotten there at your own speed, let me know. And finally to stage 5, let me know when you're there. And now go back to stage 1. [*Repeat the process*]

Randomize the Sequence

After the sequence has been reinforced in a straightforward, linear manner, the actual scrambling can begin. That is, the progression is no longer a linear one from 1 to 2 to 3 to 4 to 5; instead, the sequences are scrambled in a completely random order. (There are five factorial or 120 possible permutations for the 5 stages.) It is important that the client be instructed to move from one stage to another without *passing through* the intermittent stages. For example, when going from stage 2 to stage 5, he is told to do so without passing through stages 3 and 4. This will ensure that the stages are retrieved independently, without following the usual sequence. After passing through a few new sequences, the randomizing will become easier for the client and the therapist ought to find that he or she can proceed more rapidly with each new ordering. Eventually, the sequences can be "piggy-backed" in a more complex manner so that the client is told, "Now, go from 3 to 5 and then to 2, and give me the signal when you have completed that portion of the sequence."

At times, the anxiety accompanying each stage will produce physical alterations in the client that are clearly observable. These alterations will add confirmation to the validity of the ideomotor signals being given by the client. The entire concept of the actual Scrambling phase might be presented as follows:

> And I mentioned that so many countries have been helped by the agricultural knowledge about the ability to get minerals replenished in the soil by

rotation of the crops. You don't really have a conscious appreciation of why you have this symptom in your life. I often find it necessary to take those kitchen drawers that have become the repository for a variety of junk and organize them all into little piles in little places, so that I can mess it all up again and redo it! Every time I write a paper I have a lot of good ideas. It served me well to get them out on paper. But other times, I cut and paste the organization of those paragraphs, the sentences of those paragraphs, find a better arrangement of all those parts. And although most people only use one certain posture during the day, every practitioner of yoga realizes that the recombination of muscle tension and relaxation in different postures provides a better balance, a better understanding of the self. So it's for very good reasons that I'm going to suggest we try different combinations of the stages of the symptom. And your conscious mind really can't appreciate what your unconscious really can learn.

In your own version of crop rotation, I am still going to require the signal as we proceed in a different order. I'd like you to start with stage 3 without going through 1 and 2. When you can find that stimulus you identify as stage 3, give me the signal. And proceed directly to stage 1 without dropping to stage 2. Give me the signal again. And as quickly as possible go to stage 5 without passing through your intermittent experiences. And drop to stage 4. And go to stage 2 without passing 3, without collecting 200 dollars.

And now, unknown to you, some new arrangement of understanding is beginning to take place. And it's so subtle, you really should try a different combination. Start with stage 2 and go to stage 1. And now jump to stage 5. Then go to stage 3 and find stage 4. That shouldn't be too hard. Now let's start with stage 2 and go from 2 to 4 without passing 3. And then go to 3; and then go to 5 without passing 4. And now follow to stage 1. And in learning, it may take some time to recognize how to make sense of reexperiencing. Open-ended suggestion has a logic of assuming that there is a changing balance in a person's state; the physiology is altered in some small way so that finding a new balance may take a moment. I hope you are comfortable while you're off balance. Now let's go to stage 4 directly. And go to 5. Drop to 2 and go to 3. Drop to 1.

And I don't know if you realize whether or not it would be the factorial, the five-factorial possible permutations. That's 120. And we have a ways to go before we try all these possible combinations. Only somebody who had a math background could understand, but you can understand going directly to stage 2, dropping into stage 1, going into stage 4, dropping back to stage 3. There is something humorous about that, maybe when you go to stage 5. Now we only have 116 to go.

So maybe we should start with 1 and go to 2, go to 5, drop back to 4, go to 3, now go to 1, and go up to 4. Do you know the mathematical combinations that would be necessary going back to 3—if we'd only make a six-piece procedure instead of a five-piece procedure? Now drop back to 2. It's staggering. And it would be easier to go to 5, and just leave it at the five-step procedure, because we'd only have 113 to do to cover all possible combinations. Have we begun with stage 1 and gone to stage 4? Let's try that. And now drop to stage 2; go to stage 3; and let's just fake out and go to stage 1 before we go to stage 5.

Replacing Symptom with Resource

After directing the client to experience the new Scrambled sequences, the client will either have a great deal of confusion about the purpose of the task, or will become bored with the ease of the task. At this point, the final phase of the Scramble Technique can be initiated. The process of examining new sequences will become a tedious ordeal so that the suggestion to discard it and resolve the difficulty by returning to the previously retrieved resource will be welcomed.

> You are probably waiting for the moment when I'm going to suggest it would be easier to drop the whole thing and just go back to that feeling of success and pride in having completed a job well done; or perhaps the feeling of relaxation or dissociation you accomplished. Your conscious mind can have the feeling of relaxation and your unconscious can maintain the dissociation; or maybe your conscious mind is preparing to have a feeling of success in a job well done while your unconscious has the feeling of pride. It wouldn't be necessary for your conscious mind to go all the way to a feeling of pride while you have a dissociation and relaxation. And we have a job well done.
>
> I don't know if you realize that we have a job well done unless you have a feeling of pride associated with that relaxation while maintaining a slight dissociation. Perhaps you won't have a feeling of a job well done until you have a feeling of dissociation. And your unconscious can have pride in the relaxation that you accomplished. It makes more sense to have a feeling of pride in the job well done, while your unconscious has relaxation associated with that dissociation. It's hard to determine whether or not it's illogical to suggest that you'd have pride associated with the feeling of dissociation.

Reorientation

During the reorientation stage my goals are to complete the trance and test the success of the work as soon as possible. In this particular case, the client's ability to sustain changes after the trance was linked to the concept of "logical contradictions" and then tested by asking him to discover if he could create a logical contradiction and then resolve it. This was demonstrated by his arm levitation as he came out of trance.

In the transcription that follows I chose the concept of "oxymoron" to bring into his awareness three ideas: 1) it seems like a contradiction to keep his hands in trance and yet ask him to be out of trance; 2) he and I were contradictions in terms of our contrasting physical appearance and grooming; and 3) it was a way to say something thought-provoking about the contradiction of breathing with effort and breathing with ease.

> That sounds like an oxymoron. Some people don't know what an oxymoron is. An oxymoron is something that is a logical contradiction, like *jumbo shrimp*,

or *pretty bad*, or a *terribly wonderful* time. So to associate a dissociation with pride really is a logical contradiction. So many times a scramble experience is terribly wonderful. I hope breathing easy is not an oxymoron for you. There's no reason to have a logical contradiction about breathing easy.

It's really a lot of fun to watch you smile with your mustache. And I've enjoyed this trance greatly, so I hate to bring it to an end too soon. But there is a logical conclusion to a logical contradiction. Sooner or later, you are going to have to come out of trance.

Sooner or later you will levitate that right arm, even though it has the weight of a bracelet. We could make an oxymoron out of this trance by having you go into trance and levitate while your mind came out of the trance. Now, you really want to know how your hand can levitate up at the same speed that you come out of a trance? [*Hand and arm begins to levitate*] And you can come out of trance as a mind and be in trance as a body?

I'll tell you what I'm wondering. I'm real glad that you succeeded in overcoming something that was a weighty hand. I'm wondering whether or not, when you come out of trance as a mind, if you are going to laugh about the oxymoron we've established. I told you we could go to a party as an oxymoron. You did laugh. How does it feel?

C: [*With arm still levitated*] Incredible.

S: You could tell people you were an oxymoron. Have you ever been out of trance this way?

C: No, I never have.

S: *Never* have? So maybe this moment's not real. It's unreal.

C: In many ways, it is.

S: I noticed that you're not looking at the hand. Does it feel like it's unattached?

C: [*Laughs*] No.

S: How long do you think you can keep it that way?

C: Probably forever.

S: Probably forever. But I don't think you will keep it that way forever. Now, the best way to satisfy the need to get everything congruent is probably to drop back into a trance a little bit, catch up with yourself, and come out of trance properly, at your own speed. And now you won't be a logical contradiction anymore. [*With humorous tone*] There's always sadness with the passing of a logical contradiction.

[*Seriously*] Well, thank you. This is over now.

Follow-Up

In a follow-up contact with this client a year later, he reported that his asthma continually improved after the therapy. At the time of the therapy he used an inhaler twelve times a day; now he uses it once a day, if at all. He had had the asthmatic condition since the age of three. No other intervention was begun at the point when he received the therapy.

Discussion

Several studies have shown that hypnosis combined with behavioral techniques is significantly beneficial in alleviating asthma (Kohen, Olness, Colwell, & Heimel, 1984; Milne, 1982; Moorefield, 1971; Hypnosis for Asthma, 1968). However, this paper is intended to illustrate the Scramble Technique and not considerations of the treatment of asthma. Nevertheless, it introduces the need for an additional precautionary and ethical note about asthma treatment.

Perhaps due to notable chemical differences in victims of status asthmaticus (Kowal, Falowska, & Hanczyc, 1969), pharmacological corticosteroid therapy or artificial ventilation is often the recommended treatment (Hypnosis for Asthma, 1968). A severe, sustained, or sudden asthmatic attack or an attack resulting in hospitalization, such as status asthmaticus, requires special attention and should alter the therapist's application of this technique from the transcript displayed here. The severity of the disorder suggests extreme care when applying an intervention such as the Scramble Technique.

It is imperative that, in those cases, if the Scramble is attempted, a well-developed dissociation must be used and the Scramble Technique applied only after confirmation of the dissociation has been established. Even then, the possibility of asphyxiation due to bronchospasm in asthmaticus or status asthmaticus may be a very real possibility when stage 5 is requested. This suggests that the therapist avoid the Scramble Technique in those cases until more testing is done with such severe asthma cases.

The Scramble Technique has been used with exciting results in various cases involving extreme anxiety symptoms such as panic attacks. One noteworthy case concerned a man who had recurrent, involuntary vomiting due to anxiety. He would vomit to the point of discharging blood. This vomiting of blood occurred at a frequency of approximately three times per week and had continued for three years prior to the intervention.

The intervention was accomplished in a single hour-long session. Although the procedure was essentially similar to the above application, it was particulary interesting because of the visible signs of reverse peristalsis exhibited by the client. At times this reversal was dramatic and moving; it provided the therapist with an unusual experience of witnessing the actual effect of the treatment as it was occurring. The client's progress has been followed for four years and he has had only one partial recurrence in that time period. The one episode was so far-removed from the severity of the earlier occurrences as to be insignificant to him.

Similar reports of success occur in nearly all applications of the technique providing 1) that the symptom is related to anxiety and 2) that an incremental building in severity can be identified. It is likely that anxiety bouts that do not have this building aspect to them—that is, those which come into full intensity in an instant—will not be successfully abated by this technique.

In all treatment situations it should be remembered that choosing to intervene in a particular way at a particular time is based on a complex interaction of variables. Most often it is inappropriate to aim the therapy at the removal of the symptom without first assessing the role that is played by the symptom in the maintenance of family structure. While it is not the purpose of this paper to discuss the role symptoms play in family dynamics, the reader should be warned that an adequate assessment of such dynamics must determine the appropriate timing and choice regarding the application of this (or any) technique for symptom removal. Family members will often need to gain health-supporting mechanisms to replace the loss of a symptom. In some cases, the new mechanisms for maintaining family stability will need to be learned prior to the removal of the symptom; in other cases, the symptom will yield to therapy but will result in the acquisition of alternate mechanisms to stabilize communication and roles between family members. Often these alternate mechanisms may be viewed as various other problems. It is therefore important that therapy include guidance for the development of these substitutions during those cases when symptom removal is undertaken.

References

Erickson, M.H. (1980a). The confusion technique in hypnosis. In E.L. Rossi (Ed.), *The collected papers of Milton H. Erickson on hypnosis: Vol. I. The nature of hypnosis and suggestion* (pp. 258-291). New York: Irvington.

Erickson, M.H. (1980b). Special techniques of brief hypnotherapy. *The collected papers of Milton H. Erickson on hypnosis, Vol. IV: Innovative hypnotherapy* (pp. 149-173). New York: Irvington.

Erickson, M.H., & Rosen, H. (1980). The hypnotic and hypnotherapeutic investigation and determination of symptom-function. *The collected papers of Milton H. Erickson, on hypnosis, Vol. IV: Innovative hypnotherapy* (pp. 103-123). New York: Irvington.

Erickson, M.H., & Rossi, E.L. (1979). *Hypnotherapy: An exploratory casebook.* New York: Irvington.

Hypnosis for asthma: A controlled trial: A report to the research committee of the British Tuberculosis Association. (1968). *British Medical Journal, 1* (5223), 71-76.

Kohen, D., Olness, K., Colwell, S., & Heimel, A. (1984). The use of relaxation: Mental imagery (self-hypnosis) in the management of 505 pediatric behavioral encounters. *Journal of Developmental & Behavioral Pediatrics, 5* (1), 21-25.

Kowal, G., Falowska, A., & Hanczyc, H. (1969). Activity of salivary muramidase in allergic bronchial asthma. *Polish Medical Journal, 8,* 584-588.

Lankton, S. (1985). Multiple embedded metaphor and diagnosis. *Ericksonian psychotherapy, Vol. 1: Structures* (pp. 171-195). New York: Brunner/Mazel.

Lankton, S., & Lankton, C. (1983). *The answer within: A clinical framework of Ericksonian hypnotherapy.* New York: Brunner/Mazel.

Lankton, S., & Lankton, C. (1986). *Enchantment and intervention in family therapy: A teaching seminar on Ericksonian approaches.* New York: Brunner/Mazel.

Madanes, C. (1984). *Behind the one-way mirror.* San Francisco: Jossey-Bass.

Medicine Today: Drugs in the treatment of asthma. (1968). *British Medical Journal, 2* (5607), 750-751.

Milne, G. (1982). Hypnobehavioural medicine in a university counselling centre. *Australian Journal of Clinical & Experimental Hypnosis, 10* (1), 13-26.

Minuchin, S. (1974). *Families and family therapy.* Cambridge, MA: Harvard University Press.

Moorefield, C. (1971). The use of hypnosis and behavior therapy in asthma. *American Journal of Clinical Hypnosis, 13* (3), 162-168.

Hypnotherapy with Chronic Pain: An Ecosystemic Approach

William J. Matthews, Ph.D., and Ralph M. Daniel, Ph.D.

There is a significant amount of both experimental and clinical litera-ture detailing the use of hypnosis in the treatment of pain. For the in-dividual experiencing it, pain, from Milton Erickson's perspective, is a complex composed of remembered pain, the pain sensation in the present, and the future anticipated pain. When considered as a com-plex with a number of variables, the technique of hypnosis can be helpful in altering the perception of any one of the variables and therefore change the experience of the complex as a whole. Ad-ditionally, pain can be considered an aspect of communication be-tween individuals. In this context, pain may have a regulatory function between individuals or may reinforce a set of beliefs that any two or more individuals have come to share. The purpose of this article is to consider an Ericksonian hypnotic approach to the treatment of pain within the ecosystemic context of a couple or family. Specifically, a case of chronic pain is presented in which hypnosis occurs with both members of a married couple present. This case study is presented within the context of a larger systemic concept.

The use of hypnosis has been well documented in the treatment of both acute and chronic pain (Hilgard & Hilgard, 1975). Experimental inves-tigations have contributed detailed analyses of the parameters of the effect of hypnosis and of its underlying mechanisms (Kihlstrom, 1985). The relationship between measured hypnotic responsiveness and the capacity of the technique to reduce pain in the laboratory has been demonstrated

Address reprint requests to: William J. Matthews, Ph.D., Counseling Psychology Program, School of Education, University of Massachusetts, Amherst, Mass., 01003.

repeatedly (Shor & From, 1979). Clinical case reports discussing the use of hypnosis in reducing pain are numerous (Barber, 1982; Lassner, 1964; Melzack & Perry, 1975), but such laboratory studies and clinical reports focus exclusively on the individual who is experiencing the pain.

The more traditional approach to the hypnotic control of pain focuses on the pain itself in the treatment process. Thus, direct suggestions are typically given to the patient to ignore the pain, dissociate from the pain, have amnesia for it, feel something differently in its place, modify it, or substitute for it. As previous research cited above has indicated, there has been a great deal of clinical success with this approach. The purpose of this article is to present an hypnotic approach that considers pain a composite or construct, rather than a single noxious entity. In addition, the experience of this pain construct will be placed within the client's social system (ecosystem) and considered from the point of view of its meaning within the ecosystem.

Pain as a Construct

According to Kihlstrom (1985), "laboratory research on pain reveals that the experience has two components: (a) sensory pain, which informs the person of the location and extent of insult, injury, or disease, and (b) suffering, which has to do with the meaning of pain to the person" (p. 392). In a similar fashion, Erickson (Erickson & Rossi, 1979; Rossi, Ryan, & Sharp, 1983) has indicated that "pain is a complex, a construct, composed of past remembered pain, of present pain experience, and of anticipated pain in the future. Thus, immediate pain is augmented by past pain and enhanced by the future possibilities of pain" (Erickson in Erickson & Rossi, 1979, pp. 95-96). From these perspectives, the immediate physiologic results of harmful stimuli constitute only a central third of the entire pain experience.

Erickson and Rossi (1979) have suggested that because pain is a construct composed of different components (frequency, intensity, duration, emotion, etc.), it is more susceptible to an hypnotic treatment modality than it might be were it only a one-dimensional event located in the present. Each aspect of pain has its own associations, experiences, and expectancies and these increase the number of facets available for effective hypnotic intervention. It is important to consider that repeated pain in a particular area may come to generalize the feeling of pain to all sensations associated with that area. In fact, the original pain may be gone, but because the painful associations with a given area have now been learned, a habit may have developed that can lead to mistaken somatic disorders which may be perceived as painful.

In connection with such learned negative associations is the idea of iatrogenic disorder in which the belief in one's illness or pain by another person (often a physician, a spouse, or the self) helps create the context for, and the experience of, illness. The iatrogenic etiology of disease is an important concept because its converse, the iatrogenisis of health, is therefore implied and can be utilized. Erickson elegantly demonstrated the iatrogenisis of health with a client who complained of pain in an amputated limb. Erickson suggested to the client, "Now if you have phantom pain in a limb, you may also have phantom good feelings. And they are delightful" (Erickson & Rossi, 1979, p. 107).

While the psychological aspects of pain permit its conceptual change when it no longer serves a useful purpose, the physiological function of pain as a protective mechanism cannot be overlooked. The physical discomfort evoked by pain motivates the client to protect painful areas, to avoid stimuli causing the discomfort, and to seek help. However, because of the protective character of pain, one can develop certain psychological and emotional responses that may eventually lead to psychosomatic disturbances through the undue prolongation of such protective mechanisms (Erickson in Erickson & Rossi, 1979, p.96). This process may be the result of "secondary gain" when there is greater reinforcement in having pain than there is in not having pain (e. g., when an individual may lose disability coverage should pain diminish). Again, it is those psychological components of a pain experience which no longer includes a useful physiological component which are amenable to hypnosis.

Finally, as Erickson pointed out, clients who interpret their subjective pain experience in terms of different sensations present to the hypnotherapist many opportunities to offer to the client a reinterpretation of those various sensations. For example, a throbbing pain can be utilized by the hypnotist to suggest variations in the intensity, duration, and frequency of the throbbing or to emphasize the "comfort" that the client had ignored between throbs (Erickson & Rossi, 1979). This important application in Ericksonian work has been conceived (Lankton & Lankton, 1983) as follows: If an aspect of behavior is too complex to change as a whole, then it needs to be broken down into its component parts and such a principle is particularly relevant to the pain complex. By reducing the pain complex to its component parts, more points for intervention can be created within the painful experience, thereby increasing the probability that by changing one or more aspects of the pain complex, the experience as a whole will be moderated.

Pain as Communication Within the Ecosystem

An important addition to the above thesis is that the experience of pain is an aspect of communication between two or more individuals. While an individual is experiencing discomfort at the internal physiological level, he or she is also interacting with the environment and communicating that discomfort to another person (doctor, family member, friend, co-worker, etc.). In this instance, the expression of the experience of pain, as with any other behavior, becomes a way of communicating with those individuals who belong to the suffering person's ecosystem.

There are, of course, many ways to describe the individual within a system. Lankton and Lankton (1983) describe the individual as being composed of two basic interactive parts: 1) the private self composed of various systems—biological/chemical, muscular, emotional, cognitive (beliefs-thoughts-images, etc.). Also, part of the private self is the self-image system which is composed of past learnings, ongoing experiences, values, and expected or hoped for goals; and 2) the public self which is usually composed of a wide range of behavioral manifestations including task-related behaviors, intimacy behaviors, social-role behaviors, and such behavioral sequences as overt symptomatic behaviors.

Each of the public aspects of the self are expressed within various social contexts such as the family of origin, culture, ethnicity, employment system, social network, and so forth. For a married couple (as in the present case study), each individual brings a personal systemic experience and these combine to form the larger couple system. Within this larger system, pain can become a way for individuals to communicate with each other. Pain may have some meaning or value within the ecosystem (couple, family, friends, etc.) that supports its existence.

However, what is of importance is that pain be considered both a complex construct with past, present, and future components experienced by an individual as a unity, and an aspect of communication between two or more individuals. The experience of pain, therefore, is not only particular to the client but is also part of the ecosystem in which the client interacts with others. Therapy which intervenes both at the individual level (the experience of pain) and at the ecosystemic level (pain as communication) is much more likely to have a positive outcome.

The following case study demonstrates our approach to the management of pain in which pain as a self-construct and as a communication is utilized in working with a client and his spouse.

A Pain in the Foot: A Step Toward Dependence

Bob (pseudonym) came into therapy seeking hypnosis for the pain he experienced in his feet. He was 60 years old, married with two grown children who were no longer at home. Bob was a professional artist and

his wife worked in human services. Both reported and showed great satisfaction with their relationship and both displayed a strong sense of humor
about life in general.

Bob periodically reported a "squeezing, burning, throbbing sensation"
in his hands and predominantly in his feet as a result of frostbite suffered
in WWII. At that time, he suffered gangrene and had undergone surgical
amputation of part of one toe and removal of ligaments in two others. Bob
reported that the pain was particularly noticeable during the spring and
fall and on humid days.

When he experienced pain, Bob said he "felt like crawling into a hole."
During these periods he would sleep more than usual and drink alcohol to
excess. Bob did not take any medication for his discomfort. He felt embarrassed for showing the above behavior. However, he and his wife
reported having "good sex" even when his feet were hurting him. When he
was in pain, Mary (pseudonym) was able to help him. They joked about
"Florence Nightingale emerging." Bob indicated that he had difficulty in
asking for help from his wife when he was not in pain. Previous treatment
had included acupuncture and heating pads, both of which had been of
limited value.

Diagnosis and Treatment Goals

The diagnostic categories and treatment goals developed by Lankton
and Lankton (1983) provided a useful approach to the organization of this
case. These authors suggest the following diagnostic categories as an aid
to planning one's treatment approach: the status of the client's social network, stage of development of the client's family, stage of development of
the client, resources available to the client for change and for role flexibility, and perceptual sensitivity of the client. Based on these diagnostic
categories, treatment goals become positive changes in affect, behavior, attitude, self-image, social network, and increased enjoyment of life.

Bob and Mary had a healthy relationship and social network. Bob
needed only to be able to depend on Mary (who was quite willing) a little
more during his bouts with pain. Bob's self-concept facilitated easy and
graceful social interactions. The overall treatment plan was:

1. Elicit and frame the necessary safeguards such that pain that is adaptive can be useful and that which is not will diminish.
2. Use age regression to amplify Bob's memory of delightful walking and
   comfort prior to the onset of pain.
3. Facilitate an attitude change towards understanding that it is all right
   to have a feeling of pride for wartime experience that is not linked to

pain and that this proud feeling can be remembered independent of feeling pain.
4. Render legitimate Bob's dependency on Mary for support.
5. Suggest posthypnotically that these changes will continue indefinitely.

Treatment Approach

The treatment method used the multiple-embedded metaphor model (Lankton & Lankton, 1983; Matthews & Dardeck, 1984) to create the opportunity for the new learnings proposed by the treatment plan to occur. The multiple-embedded metaphor uses an interlocking series of metaphorical stories, designed with the client in mind, to access needed resources contained within the client in order to produce therapeutic change. The pattern for the multiple-embedded metaphor is as follows:

A1. Hypnotic Induction based on utilization principles.
    B1. Begin a story that matches the client's situation.
        C1. Develop resources and/or trance phenomena that will be useful in the resolution of the problem.
            D. Directing experience—usually focusing on the presenting problem
        C2. Link previously developed resources to the social network for symptom change.
    B2. End matching metaphor often focusing on the next developmental stage of the client.
A2. Reorient to waking state—use of posthypnotic suggestions to support permanent change.

The major function of this format is that it presents material to the client in an indirect manner in trance, material that he or she might otherwise find difficult to consciously accept. The use of multiple stories presents the opportunity for the client to: 1) increase the depth of trance as he or she attempts to track all the stories and their meanings; 2) reexperience previous skills and resources; and 3) thereby achieve new learnings, perceptions, and behaviors in relationship to the presenting problem. Recent research (Mosher & Matthews, 1985) has provided some initial laboratory support for Lankton and Lankton's (1983) belief that this format increases amnesia for the specific material by the client, thereby facilitating its potential for therapeutic effect.

Session One

In all of the treatment sessions, Mary was present. In session one, induction proceeded smoothly utilizing indirect suggestions as discussed by

Lankton and Lankton (1983) and Erickson and Rossi (1979; 1980). Specifically, conscious/unconscious dissociation suggestions were made to Bob in order that he might begin to consider that his conscious mind has limitations that are not relevant for his unconscious mind. For example, he was told, "Your conscious mind, Bob, wonders how you will learn to feel comfort in your feet, while your unconscious mind can remember that good feeling of warmth or heaviness." The goal of the induction was twofold: 1) to promote a trance experience that would create an expectancy for positive change, and 2) to help Bob experience a number of sensations that he had perhaps forgotten or not associated with his feet and hands. Bob showed a number of ideomotor responses that were interpreted by the authors as indicating a medium level of trance depth (e.g., breathing rate change, cheeks flattening, eye closure, reduced movement, and hand levitation).

Matching metaphor (B1). The first story that Bob was told concerned a Boy Scout on his first winter camping trip with his friends and their fathers. Bob was told how the Boy Scout awoke to find his boots frozen, and himself wet and cold. The initial part of the story discussed how the Boy Scout, while not enjoying the physical difficulties of the experience, thoroughly enjoyed the camaraderie of the trip—learning to survive in a hostile environment and to stand on your own two feet even when your boots were frozen. The joys of building a fire, the warmth of cooking and sharing food with friends, of learning to tie knots and asking for help in untying them were all discussed in some detail.

Resource metaphor (C1). The resource metaphor in this session focused on the issue of dependency. Bob had said that he found it difficult to ask directly for support from Mary when his pain increased. Our belief was that if he were able to ask for help during the time of his discomfort, the experience of pain would be modified by his wife's care-giving. Thus, two elaborate stories emphasizing the positive value of dependency were told. In the first, a detailed story of Michelangelo and his need to depend on his family, friends, benefactors, stone cutters, and so forth was presented to the client. The theme of dependency was emphasized in great detail both at the cognitive and at the physiological level (the affect associated with feeling dependent). This was done so that Bob would have both levels of meaning associated with dependency, thereby facilitating his experience of dependency in trance.

The second story also emphasized the theme of dependency, in a slightly altered way. The client was told of a therapist's (second author) experience with another client who had a restaurant in which she liked to help her customers with choices from the menu. She took great pleasure in being able to suggest meals that her customers would enjoy. Bob was told, through the story, of the joys and satisfactions (in detail at both the physiological and cognitive level) of sometimes having things done for one.

Direct work (D). In the direct work phase of the multiple-embedded metaphor structure, the hypnotic phenomenon of age regression was utilized in order to create the opportunity for Bob to reexperience a time when he had no pain in his feet. Subsequently, a reframe of the pain experience was offered in trance: Bob was told that the sensations in his feet were actually an early barometer of the changing seasons, and that he could take pleasure in knowing about those changing seasons long before other people knew about them.

Following the reframe, the work focused directly on Bob's pain. Age regression was used to create the opportunity for Bob to reexperience the effectiveness of his acupuncture treatment. This age regression also served as a catalyst for earlier age regression to a time prior to the injury to his feet (i.e., as a teenager). Suggestions were given to Bob that he could have those good feelings any time he wanted them. The theme presented to him was that his hands and feet could stay regressed with those good feelings while he enjoyed the present.

Linking of resources (C2). After the direct work, the story about Michelangelo begun earlier (C1) was completed. The emphasis was on his accomplishments, the feeling of pride, standing tall, completing work, and the satisfaction of depending on others to give help. These accomplishments were associated with typical events in the protagonist's (and therefore the client's) everyday life (touching paint brushes, walking into the studio, etc.) such that these events or stimuli would come to evoke the positive feelings developed in the trance. Important in this part of the trance work was not only to link the cognitive associations to common stimuli but also the physiological components.

Finish matching metaphor (B2). At this point, the therapist returned to and completed the original story about the Boy Scout. Bob was told how much the child did enjoy the warm bath that his mother had poured for him upon arrival home from the camping trip and how nice it was to be able to let her take care of him in that way. The themes of comfort and dependency were emphasized in the conclusion of the story. In addition, future developmental themes were also emphasized; for example, the Boy Scout would look back on the camping trip with a sense of pride and accomplishment, and the learnings, not obvious at the time, would be drawn upon at a later period in his life. Developmental themes of aging, children growing and leaving home, and the different comforts and pleasures that one experiences over time were touched upon in the completion of the matching metaphor.

Reorientation (A2). Bob's reorientation from trance occurred smoothly and was based on the induction procedure used with him. During reorientation the focus was shifted back to Bob's initial trance experiences (eye closure, hand levitation, his wife's responses, etc.). Thus, the conscious/ unconscious distinctions were emphasized along with the feelings and sensations of warmth and heaviness discussed earlier. The entire trance experience was ratified so as to create an expectancy for future change. At the conclusion of the session, Bob was given a homework assignment to ask "Florence Nightingale" to massage his feet for 10 minutes four times during the next two weeks. He was told to ask her particularly when he was not experiencing pain in his feet.

Session Two

During the two-week interim, Bob reported that he felt significantly less pain than he had felt prior to the last session. Both Bob and Mary had enjoyed the homework assignment and made a humorous comment about "Florence Nightingale" being available. Bob indicated that he had never thought about asking for help from Mary in the way that he had to do in order to carry out his homework assignment. The planned goals for session two remained the same as those in session one, that is, to create an opportunity for couple restructuring around the legitimate need for dependency and to use hypnotic phenomena, such as for dissociation, for the specific reduction of pain.

Induction (A1). As a lead-in to trance induction, the therapist used an indirect suggestion for the development of trance when he suggested, "Why don't you write a check to me now, while you still can?" In writing the check, Bob had developed an expectancy for trance and began to show trance behaviors on his own. This expectancy was also true for Mary, as evidenced by her trance behaviors. The therapist utilized this spontaneous trance behavior to help Bob reach a medium level of trance depth.

Matching metaphor (B1). The goal in this initial metaphor was to suggest some restructuring around the issue of dependency and the legitimacy of having one's needs met. Hence, a story was begun which centered on a couple who hiked up the Pawnee Pass in the Rockies with everything they would need to survive in the wilderness. They started at two different prearranged points and zig-zagged up the mountain. By zig-zagging they were able to come together at different times on their journey. This story went on to describe the hardships and difficulties of the journey and the joys of meeting each other when each seemed to need it most. The therapist said that at one point when the couple felt like giving up, they saw a troop of Girl Scouts go by and then they knew that they could make it. Both Bob and Mary chuckled at this point in the trance. The indirect suggestion was offered that sometimes there can be humor in life's hardships.

Resource metaphor (C1). The goal in the resource metaphor was to enhance Bob's ability to experience dissociation in connection with his pain. Erickson and Rossi (1979), as well as Lankton and Lankton (1983), consider dissociation a powerful technique to employ to reduce the sensation of pain. To help him develop a dissociative experience, Bob was told about a woman who experienced floating out of her body, as if she were a light butterfly, while giving birth to her child. Care was taken by the therapist to describe the dissociative experience of the protagonist such that Bob, in order to understand the story he was listening to, would develop his own dissociative experience (Rossi, in Erickson & Rossi, 1980).

Direct work (D). In this section of the multiple-embedded metaphor structure with dissociation secured, the therapist had Bob review a number of his own difficult life experiences without the emotional feelings (i.e., the pain) attached to these events. This was done in order that he might create a different perspective from which to regard his experiences. He was told to review these experiences as if he were watching himself watching a movie, removed from the experience itself. The therapist then began to describe a number of common experiences in which a range of emotions could be observed by Bob. These included the feeling of sadness, excitement, fear, and satisfaction. The therapist was careful in his observation of Bob during the descriptions of the various feeling states in order to verify that Bob would remain dissociated. Bob remained calm, relaxed, and comfortable throughout this period and this behavior provided strong feedback to the therapist that he was dissociated from the pain which normally would have been associated with those experiences described.

Linking resources (C2). At this point, the previously accessed resources were linked to a self-image protocol (Lankton & Lankton, 1983). This protocol provides the client (in a relationship with a significant other) with an opportunity to view him or herself with the desired feelings, affect, attitude, and behaviors to undergo a situation in which they will be of use (i.e., the social network, or the context in which the discomfort occurs). This particular client was told a story about a man who changed from solo bobsledding to team bobsledding, and the ensuing enjoyment was described through the rhythm, flow, speed, and feeling of comfort derived from being able to depend on his team. Finally, Bob was reminded of the experience of riding on a bus and dreamily seeing one's reflection in the window and how this reflection could change into scenes and pictures reminiscent of tender and dependent moments. Bob was told in some detail about the bus rider's experience of seeing himself with all the positive attributes (good feelings in the absence of pain, ability to be dependent on another, etc.) he desired. There were a number of scenarios focusing on the protagonist of the story (the bus rider), through which Bob could experience himself, in relation to others having those good feelings. These scenarios ranged from such simple scenes as brushing one's teeth, riding in a car, and walking down the street, to more complex scenes such as talking with one's spouse after a difficult day, enjoying a rest by taking "a load off your feet," and so forth.

Finishing matching metaphor (B2). The intent of the therapist was to suggest future changes that might be expected to occur (e.g., Bob and Mary continuing to mature together). The story of the mountain-climbing couple was resumed with their descent of the mountain. Bob and Mary were told how that couple stopped at various points on the way down (e.g., by a lake) and how they reflected on different aspects of their achievement together at one stop, while at another they discussed their future. Long after that journey, when they looked in their attic and saw their hiking equipment, they were reminded of their "incredible feat." Again, interspersed between the details of the protagonists' relationship were indirect suggestions for changes in Bob and Mary's relationship.

Reorientation (A2). The reintroduction of the "here and now" followed a process similar to that of the previous trance session. There was an emphasis on conscious amnesia for much of the work done so that the unconscious mind could provide the changes that they desired. At the conclusion of the trance work, the couple was given another homework assignment in which Bob was asked to draw a picture of his pain and to give it to his wife stating, "Thank you for being who you are." Mary, who played guitar and sang, was instructed to write and perform a song for "Bob and his pain."

Session Three

The couple returned for a final session as follow-up to the hypnotic work and to the homework assignments. Bob reported a significant reduction in his discomfort and an increase in movement toward Mary during times of discomfort. He was intrigued by the assignment given to him and produced a powerful picture of a man with a huge hole in his middle carrying a heavy pack with spring mousetraps on his hands and feet. He reported that in giving the picture to Mary, the pain was significantly reduced. Mary produced a delightful tune which she sang in the session. The song said that Bob had felt an injunction from his parents to block and to reject any positive feelings he had toward his WWII experiences. Bob responded with humor to the challenge of whether or not he could enjoy his wartime memories without pain. With reference to the hypnotic work, Bob reported that he did remember some story about a pack of Boy Scouts and that he felt somehow "positive about it."

In this last session, Bob was given one more homework assignment, an ambiguous task (i. e., a task whose purpose is left to the client to determine and which the client incorrectly assumes the therapist has full knowledge of [Lankton & Lankton, 1983]). He was told to carry around a knapsack, filled with rocks, every day for a week and to put in or take out of it the number of rocks that seemed appropriate. A two-week follow-up revealed that Bob continued to experience less pain than he had before the treatment. He had rated his pain at the beginning of our work at a "5" on a 10-point imaginary scale (10 represents extreme pain) and at follow-up revealed that it was consistently at a "1."

Bob related that he and Mary had taken a trip to a large city where he walked a great deal but experienced only minor soreness in his feet. Mary noticed that the knapsack assignment seemed to have had some particular meaning for Bob. On the trip Bob had wanted to see a WWII plane, and he needed to lighten the load he was carrying in order to do so. Mary attributed Bob's willingness to ease his burden to the knapsack assignment. As of this writing (six months post-therapy), Bob continues to report significant pain reduction, particularly in his feet.

Conclusions

The foregoing case report illustrates the importance of considering 1) pain as a construct (i.e., the remembered, present, and anticipated aspects of pain) and 2) the client within his or her social context or network. To have intervened with Bob without considering his wife's role in his pain experience would have been, in our opinion, a mistake which might have unnecessarily complicated and prolonged treatment. The use of the multiple-embedded metaphor structure enabled the therapy to address both the social matrix in which the pain occurred, as well as the pain experience itself. Our treatment approach facilitated the altering of an experience of pain within the context in which it occurred—the marital relationship. The metaphors were chosen to focus on the theme of dependence (coming together for comfort and support) as well as to alter the pain experience itself.

It is interesting to note that while the trance was ostensibly intended for Bob, Mary consistently showed trance behavior at the same time (eye closure, flattening of the cheeks, reduced movement, etc.). Her behavior demonstrated that she, too, was engaged in an unconscious search for meaning which resulted in new behavior (Rossi, in Erickson & Rossi, 1980). The use of trance directed toward Bob with Mary present allowed for a different pattern of behavior to evolve between the couple. That trance became a shared experience of comfort between the two and later may have served as an unconscious endorsement for the evolution of different patterns of behavior. For Bob, Mary became directly associated with comfort.

In summary, we considered that the success of treatment in this case of chronic pain can be attributed to the understanding of pain as both a construct (i.e., composed of historical, present, and anticipated sensations) and an aspect of communication with the client's ecosystem. To ignore the larger system in which pain occurs and to restrict the therapeutic intervention to the physical aspect (one individual's personal experience) is to fractionate the ecosystem in a way that, in our opinion, may reduce the probability of a successful outcome.

References

Barber, J. (1982). *Psychological approaches to management of pain.* New York: Brunner/Mazel.

Erickson, M., & Rossi, E. (1979). *Hypnotherapy: An exploratory casebook.* New York: Irvington.

Erickson, M., & Rossi, E. (1980). *The collected works of Milton H. Erickson, M.D. (Vol. 1).* New York: Irvington.

Hilgard, E., & Hilgard, J. (1975). *Hypnosis in the relief of pain.* Los Angeles: Kaufman.

Kihlstrom, J. (1985). Hypnosis. *Annual Review of Psychology, 36,* 385-418.

Lankton, S., & Lankton, C. (1983). *The answer within: A clinical framework for Ericksonian hypnotherapy.* New York: Brunner/Mazel.

Lassner, J. (Ed.). (1964). *Hypnosis in anesthesiology.* New York: Springer-Verlag.

Matthews, W., & Dardeck, K. (1984). The construction of metaphor in the counseling process. *AMCHA Journal, 7,* 11-24.

Melzack, R., & Perry, C. (1975). Self-regulation of pain: Use of alpha feedback and hypnotic training for control of chronic pain. *Experimental Neurology, 46,* 452-469.

Mosher, D., & Matthews, W. (1985). *Structural amnesia in hypnosis.* Paper under review.

Rossi, E., Ryan, M., & Sharp, F. (Eds.). (1983). *Healing in hypnosis by Milton H. Erickson.* New York: Irvington.

Shor, R., & From, E. (1979). *Hypnosis: Developments in research and new perspectives.* New York: Adline.

Therapeutic Metaphor in the Treatment of Childhood Asthma: A Systemic Approach

Carol J. Kershaw, Ed.D.

This article describes the use of Ericksonian hypnotherapy with an asthmatic child to produce symptom reduction and change in the pattern of family interaction. Following hypnotherapy, the asthmatic boy experienced fewer asthmatic attacks per week and was able to manage the symptoms with less medication. The mother was freed from the burden of constantly monitoring her son's behavior. In addition, the parents began to spend time together as a couple rather than orienting their relationship around the asthmatic child.

Children who suffer from asthma tend to be highly sensitive to certain environmental and psychological stressors. Several studies cited below have examined these stressors, as well as various treatment modalities, and suggest that asthma can be adjunctively treated through the use of hypnotherapy. Why this change can be created is not clear, but may include "enhancement of mastery, reduction of anxiety that may have some physiological effect, direct effects in relaxing bronchial smooth muscle, changes in parental attitudes and behavior, and resolution of unconscious conflicts" (Gardner & Olness, 1981, p. 191). Therefore, this article reviews some related literature and discusses a systemic perspective about asthma. A case study is presented which utilized the therapeutic metaphor as a treatment framework.

Address reprint requests to: Carol J. Kershaw, Ed.D., Milton H. Erickson Institute of Central Texas (Houston), 9207 Country Creek Drive, Suite, 170, Houston, TX 77036.

Asthma is a condition where the bronchial tubes become constricted, causing difficulty in breathing. This response may occur in reaction to certain allergies, exercise, change in temperature, seasons, or intense emotional responses that are created in family or other social encounters. Since there is a multietiology and a hereditary predisposition to the disease, treatment must address several aspects which include: 1) the family system; 2) how the symptom may become exacerbated; 3) individual emotional factors; 4) individual family member's reactions to the symptomatic person; 5) how the individual with the symptom manages the problem; and 6) how much influence the symptomatic person perceives having over the disease or condition.

Research literature suggests that hypnosis is a useful treatment for asthma, both with adults and children. With specific concern for the management of the asthmatic child, several studies of hypnosis have shown a significant improvement in the condition. In 1986 the British Tuberculosis Association conducted a study in which 252 patients, ages 10 to 60, were divided into two groups. One group used breathing exercises, while the other group used self-hypnosis. The hypnotic group reduced symptoms in 59%, while the control group had a reduction in symptoms of 43%. The methods reported are usually direct hypnosis with posthypnotic suggestions for control, breathing easier, and reduction of wheezing (Aronoff, Aronoff, & Peck, 1975; Collison, 1975; Barbour, 1980; Wilkinson, 1981; Conners, 1983).

In one study of 17 children, ages six to 17, direct hypnosis was used to develop easier breathing and reduction of other symptoms. Almost all of the subjects experienced improvement (Aronoff, Aronoff, & Peck, 1975, p. 361).

Other studies involving biofeedback training report reduction in symptoms and management of the disease. Usually, direct hypnotic suggestions are given concomitantly with biofeedback, although some may not refer to this as hypnosis (Feldman, 1976; Khan, 1977; Scherr & Crawford, 1978).

Erickson describes the case of a 12-year-old male asthmatic patient with whom he successfully used fractionation, a technique to gradually reduce symptoms. The therapist may encourage the patient to think about having slightly less of the symptom, such as 1%, 10%, 20% less, and so on, until the symptom significantly decreases. The boy's attitude shifted from believing that 100% of his asthma was caused by pollens to thinking that 20% was caused by pollens and 80% was caused by fear. When he learned to manage the fear, he was then able to experience fewer symptoms. The patient's asthma was acknowledged; then it was suggested that he could manage with fewer symptoms. Erickson concluded that, "You approach the correction of psychopathology by a gradual eradication of it, not by attempting to contest it, dispute it, or annihilate it" (1983, pp. 198-199).

During the last few years, a focus on stress-exacerbated and related disorders has been made by both psychologists and physicians. As a result, a single factor causation for the view of the disease is no longer appropriate (Pelletier, 1977, p. 13). These findings indicate that one must consider genetics, family constellation, environment, and individual sensitivities.

In addition, to create useful interventions, it is important to identify family dynamics. The pattern or sequence of behavior that may develop in a family with an asthmatic child often becomes as problematic as the illness itself. When the child has an asthma attack, the mother may feel frightened, anxious, and hover over the child. As the mother increases her involvement with her child, the father may feel abandoned by his wife, and he may withdraw from the child or take the illness lightly.

The child's illness may raise the father's fears of having a child who is sickly and unable to participate in traditional father-son activities. When the father withdraws, this behavior may frighten the mother even more. She may feel abandoned in her effort to maintain her child's health. Consequently, she may overfunction and become even more involved with the child and distance herself further from the father. The couple may become less social and increasingly orient their relationship around tasks concerning the child.

The child may sense the parents' increased tension, which may be denied by the parents to avoid adding more stress to the situation. In reaction, the child's anxiety may increase. This increased anxiety may help trigger more asthma attacks or worsen others.

Frequently, the mother will view her child's increased symptoms as an indication that her increased involvement is warranted. The father may then become all the more certain that his child is developing into someone less "masculine," which he may interpret as a comment on the quality of his fathering or his own "masculinity." He may criticize the mother for her overinvolvement, and she may criticize him for his underinvolvement.

The father's movement away from the child may be an attempt to counterbalance the mother's movement toward the child. He may come to resent the child because of his grief about losing his partner to this little person. The mother may react to the father's anger unconsciously and invest even more in the child. This common systemic pattern often continues to escalate with more frequent and severe asthma attacks, greater involvement by the mother, greater withdrawal by the father, and less interaction between the parents as a marital couple. Of course, these roles may be reversed. The father may take the more nurturing role, while the mother becomes the more distant member.

Thus, each person further increases movement toward what seems to be the only logical solution to the problem. Eventually, despite increased levels of medication, the asthma attacks continue to worsen and, in some cases, may reach a life-threatening level. This pattern of behavior is cyclical, and the ensuing escalation of anger and resentment for both marital partners may lead to increased tensions in the marriage. As the couple struggles, the conflict may be driven underground and denied and the couple may remain together as distant partners. The movement toward each other may occur only in the demand of an asthmatic emergency, where they must cooperate to save their child's life.

Once this pattern of behavior has begun, it becomes a recursive process; a kind of repetitive dance that takes on a life of its own. Each family member's reaction to the asthma and to one another defines the system in which they operate. As Hoffman states, " . . . the problem creates the system" (1985, p. 386; 1986). For instance, parents in a support group for dealing with their asthmatic children listed a number of complaints about the problem. Among them were: 1) it disrupts life; 2) it creates demands on parental time; 3) it is a cause of divorce; 4) it is costly; 5) it creates a sense of isolation; 6) parents become overprotective and extremely cautious; 7) parents feel like prisoners in their own home; and 8) parents feel guilty for having feelings of resentment toward the child and often turn those feelings toward the other spouse (American Lung Association, 1986).

The way in which the partners manage their spousal and parental relationship in relation to the asthmatic child will be influenced by their own expectations and by the beliefs each holds concerning appropriate nurturing and caretaking of a symptomatic child. If, for example, the mother learned in her family of origin that a good mother sacrifices her own needs and the relationship with her husband for the sick child, this behavior may be repeated in the context of her child's life-threatening illness. If the father learned from his family of origin that a man is expected to function in the world regardless of pain or illness, he may maintain the same expectations of a son. If the son is the asthmatic child, we can see how personal expectations may become conflictual.

It is important for the therapist who treats a family with an asthmatic child to understand that neither the mother, the father, nor the child "causes" the difficulty in the family system. Each member may attempt to solve the problem the best way he or she knows how but may only worsen it. What is being described here is an evolving family pattern which fits together instead of a pattern where one member "causes" another to behave in a particular way. There is no use for blame in any therapeutic treatment.

Pattern interruption as well as new learnings and associations that lead to more functional behaviors are goals of Ericksonian hypnotherapy. Erickson not only targeted interventions at the level of behavioral sequences but also helped family members to retrieve needed attitude, affect, and behavioral resources that would help them achieve more comfort, control, and satisfaction in life (Lankton & Lankton, 1983). In the following case, Ericksonian hypnotherapy was utilized to interrupt a dysfunctional pattern of behavior, retrieve needed resources, and help the child gain control over his symptoms. Before describing the case, one more aspect of theory is important.

T. X. Barber (1984) has described the mind-body interaction as one which is greatly affected by the transfer of ideas from one person and accepted by another. The ideas "can be communicated to the cells of the body and to the chemicals within the cells. The cells, then, can change their activities in order to conform to the meanings or ideas which have been transmitted to them" (p. 116). In addition, Hall (1984) reported that "the literature . . . suggests that hypnosis may potentially be able to alter immune responses in order to influence the underlying biochemical factors of physical diseases" (p. 101). Kershaw (1979) and Rossi (1986) have also examined this psychophysiological interaction and concluded that the mind can heal physical illness. Consequently, we can see the importance of a multidimensional approach in treating asthma.

"Transforming Transformers"

This case concerns an eight-year-old Chinese-American boy who had asthma from the age of three. As is frequently found in families with an asthmatic member, his mother often asked him how he felt and frequently corrected his behavior. For example, she asked him to stop fidgeting. She pulled up his socks, and he pushed them down only to have her pull them up again. She reported that her son had almost died twice from asthmatic attacks and she was understandably frightened for his safety.

His father, on the other hand, was somewhat aloof and uninvolved with the family and highly skeptical of therapy in general. He adhered to the Chinese cultural norm of refraining from talking to people outside the family. The father had conflict with the mother over his son's asthmatic condition. He seemed to deny the severity of the problem to the point that he would refuse to give medication to his son. The father was invited to attend the first session. However, he refused to come to this and subsequent sessions. Consequently, the therapy was conducted with the mother and son.

In the first session, a history of medications was taken, along with a history of administering the medication, frequency of attacks, pattern of attacks, if any, and specific fears the child experienced (R. Wilson, personal communication, January 31, 1986). Discussing with the mother how both parents managed the problem was enlightening in that marital conflict seemed to be expressed through disagreement over how to manage the son's asthmatic condition. The father was hesitant to deliver medication to his son so that the mother elected to take total charge of managing the condition. Because of the situation, she indicated that she had little personal life and refrained from visiting friends in another state. In the first session, interview management became an issue and the therapist relied upon many utilizations to defuse the customary communication between the boy and his mother. For instance, in the case of the quarreling about the socks, cited above, the therapist instructed R. to leave one up for his mother and one down for himself just for the session.

In the second session, a finger thermometer was used to demonstrate to the youngster and his mother how one can influence body temperature through relaxation. Both mother and son were given the thermometer and taken through an indirect induction where suggestions of raising finger temperature were delivered. The son was able to raise his temperature, while his mother lowered hers. As a result, the son was delighted that he could do something that his mother could not, and this management mastery was used to indirectly suggest to the boy that he could manage the asthma much better without his mother's constant intervention. To demonstrate management of the asthma, the boy who asked to demonstrate how he could make himself breathe more clearly by slowing his breathing rate. He demonstrated obvious enjoyment in this procedure. He was instructed to practice breathing clearly when he had any tightness or constriction.

The young boy brought his collection of "transformers" to the therapy sessions. These are small toys such as tanks, spaceships, and cassette recorders with many moveable parts that allow the child to twist and change their appearance (or transform them) into somewhat grotesque strong men with vividly descriptive names, such as Laser Beak, Mega Tron, Sound Wave, and so forth. The child's objective in playing with these "transformers" is to alter their appearance first in one way, then another, and then back again.

R. was asked to describe the transformers in detail and to indicate which superheroes he particularly liked. Shock Wave, Iron Hide, Triple Changer, Mirage, Blue Streak, Thunder Cracker, Star Scream, and Sky Fire were some of his favorites. This therapist thought that these heroes could be worked into a metaphorical story in a later session.

The third session involved a one-hour metaphorical story, following the attitude protocol from Lankton and Lankton's model (1983, 1985, 1986), and had as goals: 1) attitude restructuring for the mother and son so that

R. could manage the asthma without her constant attention; and 2) a self-image shift for the boy to feel more in charge of his daily life, more independent and normalized with children his age. Because of the child's age and his difficulty in maintaining focused attention for a long time, a simple metaphorical story was used rather than a complete multiple-embedded metaphor.

The fourth session addressed these goals and, in addition, a family structure change so that the mother could become less involved with her son, more involved with her husband, and maintain her own life better by becoming more active outside the home.

R. had attacks three to four times per week, some being quite severe. In addition, he suffered from night terrors which were manifested in the fear of a werewolf. R. would imagine the monster stalking him in his room. The beginning of obsessional thinking could be seen developing because R. would only be able to force the werewolf to disappear by "thinking about him coming closer. If I think about his disappearing, he comes closer. If I think about his coming closer, he disappears." R. suffered from this fear every evening, which was unknown to his mother prior to the psychotherapy sessions. We worked in this paradoxical manner of having the werewolf come closer and go away in the office, and R. was able to send him away for good.

This obsessional thinking seems symbolic of, "I can get my beastly mother to finally stop plaguing me and go away only when I stop resisting her coming closer," and thereby take control of the relationship. The symptom considered in this way is an example of symptoms as metaphor.

An interesting indication of the recursive role played by the identified patient's parents is indicated in the fact that the client's mother experienced an increase in anxiety during the hours of 11 and 4 o'clock. These were the hours when R. often had asthmatic attacks. In addition, his mother would constantly check on him when he was home and stay by the phone when he was at school just in case she was needed to pick him up and take him to a physician. Consequently, the family revolved around the symptomatic child, and the mother especially felt imprisoned. To apply the recursive framework in the treatment of this family, this systemic aspect also needed to be addressed in therapy.

Stephen and Carol Lankton's (1983) elaboration of Erickson's work describes the structure of the multiple-embedded metaphor, a framework for creating specific changes in attitude, affect, and behavior. The model uses metaphorical stories, anecdotes, and symbols that parallel the client's situation in a specific structure to facilitate change within the context of strategically used trance.

"Metaphor is a way to stimulate an individual's unconscious memories and past learnings to create new solutions" (J. W. Wade, personal communication, June 10, 1986). Erickson said, "I have viewed much of what I have done as expediting the currents of change already seething within the person and the family—but currents that need the 'unexpected,' the 'illogical' and the 'sudden' move to lead them into tangible fruition" (Watzlawick, Beavin, & Jackson, 1967, p. ix). It is the metaphor which can provide the impetus toward transformative change. As a powerful instrument of communication, metaphor can address a problem at multiple levels and allow the patient to create personal meaning.

The following is a summary of both metaphorical story sessions.

The Knight Training

A long time ago, in a faraway land, lived a little boy named Tom. He lived during the time when young men trained to be knights. Tom wanted to become a knight, but he needed to attend knight school [pause] during the day. [pause] So, Tom began his journey to the castle that was outside the village where he lived. He was scheduled to meet with the knight schoolmaster who would teach him how to be a master [pause] ful (1) (k)night through knight training. He took the path that wound around through the pretty countryside. When you're out in the country like that, you find yourself taking nice, long, deep breaths, and enjoying the cool air and the sunshine that warms you deep inside. Even as you think about that now, you can have those feelings of being able to breathe deeply and fell the warmth on your chest and in your lungs.

So Tom continued walking down to the castle and finally came to the drawbridge. The knight schoolmaster let down the bridge, and Tom walked across and was welcomed to the school. Tom was so excited to be in this castle. The knight schoolmaster took him on a tour, showed him all of the rooms and the outside areas where the young men were practicing sword swinging and thrusting. Of course, the young men were learning how to slay dragons. And they had to learn exactly the right way to hold the sword, the right way to stand, and how to use the power of the breath.

Now the knight schoolmaster took Tom and invited him to join the class on dragon slaying with swords. He instructed the boys to stand balanced on both feet, to breathe by pushing your bellybutton out, and to swing the sword in a special way. This special way of standing and breathing was important when you meet a dragon in your path. And the knight schoolmaster told the boys that "when you're scared, you hold your breath, which is the opposite thing you need to do." So he had them imagine standing in front of the dragon, feeling that tightness in their chests, and then shifting their breath and breathing from the bellybutton. "This," he said, "is the power of the breath."

Then, the boys' teacher set up three different trials. Each boy had to slay three dragons to become a knight. First one dragon and then another, and each dragon was bigger than the last. Finally, it was time for Tom's big test. He was to go into the arena where the biggest, fiercest dragon was waiting to do battle. Tom was a little afraid, but he thought, "Well, I've done this twice before, and I think I can do it a third time!" He entered the arena and looked around. There he was, across the arena, a huge dragon that was breathing fire and belching smoke. Tom noticed that he started holding his breath. And so he thought, "You can remember what the knight schoolmaster said [*pause*] about standing balanced, breathing from your bellybutton, and you can feel that air going into your lungs in just the right way, and you can feel the air move back out." "This," he said, "is the power of the breath." So he stood his ground, took his sword and brought it back over his head, and just when the dragon was about to breathe fire on him, Tom cut off the dragon's head! And Tom graduated, became a knight, and went on to have many other adventures.

In this summarized story there are several embedded commands and directions about maintaining clear breathing in a stressful situation. Also, suggestions about sleeping through the night were given (knight training). Additionally, the attitude taught in this story is that one can learn how to control a natural reflex of tightening up under stress to maintain composure. The story had the boy managing this stressful situation among a class of boys. Consequently, it suggested that R. could do what other boys could do.

The Land of Breeze

A second metaphor continued to use Tom as the main protagonist who is called by the knight schoolmaster to come to the aid of the people in the Land of Breeze. Since Tom has become a master knight, he is selected by his teacher to fight the evil Count in this land. This is a beautiful country where the air blows free and easy and where you can experience the feelings of freedom and pleasure of that calm, rhythmical movement one sees and feels in the Land of Breeze.

To summarize the story, the evil Count was taxing his people so much that they had to pay for the use of their fresh air. Each time someone opened a window, he or she had to pay a fee. So, eventually all the people began to leave their windows closed. Some of the people began to feel all choked up and stifled and unable to breathe in the Land of Breeze.

Because the people stayed indoors, the land became barren. No one was taking care of it, watering and feeding the land, so it began to die.

Fortunately, Tom comes to the land and brings with him some friends, Laser Beak, Mega Tron and Shock Wave. Together they are able to beat the evil Count and turn the Land of Breeze back to the people. And the Land of Breeze once again becomes a beautiful land, where the air is again free and easy. Tom returns to his knight schoolmaster who tells him how pleased he is with him, and he now knows that Tom can take care of himself and manage quite well. His teacher says, "You carry my teaching and my voice with you wherever you go. I can now trust that you can manage without my full attention. It's so nice when you can turn your attention to other important matters, such as a trip I want to take to relax."

Within this story, suggestions are given about the ease of breathing. The evil Count represents any stress, such as problematic parental figures, and is beaten with the help of superheroes, childhood projections of strength and ability to handle difficulties. In addition, the knight schoolmaster, who is a parental figure, suggests that Tom can indeed manage on his own. He can trust that his teachings have been internalized enough for Tom to be safe. Here it can be seen that this last suggestion was directed toward the mother in order to help her become less involved. The story also included elements about the teacher being able to get back to those important tasks he needed to accomplish, as well as a long desired vacation that he could now take.

Therapy consisted of four sessions, 50 minutes each. The first session was used to gather history, make an assessment, and teach R. how to focus on his breathing to control the wheezing. This initial session also was used to develop rapport and understand the values and interests of each person. The second session consisted of more discussion about how the family system was organized around the asthmatic child and some of R.'s fears. The finger thermometer was used in this session to demonstrate how one may control the autonomic nervous system. R. took some time to explain each of the transformers and its particular superhuman strength. Sessions three and four each were designed primarily for the delivery of a therapeutic metaphor described above.

Results

After the initial session, the mother reported that her son was unable to interrupt an asthma attack at school. At home, she would find him practicing the relaxation without her mentioning it to him. He had been instructed to attempt to practice this technique without his parents' knowledge.

After the second session, the mother reported that a reduction in medication had been achieved. R. was needing medication every five to six hours, instead of every five and then three hours later. Also, R. was sleeping through the night and not needing any medication between 2 and 3 a.m., which he formerly had required. Weekly allergy injections dropped to every two weeks.

There was some reduction in the amount of medication taken and some reduction in frequency. The young boy was able to manage the condition much better and felt more in control of his own body. Also, he had fewer asthmatic attacks, which dropped from several per week to one every two weeks to, finally, one every three weeks according to the referring physician (F. Hill and D. Hill, personal communication, June 10, 1986). The child's school attendance increased to approximately three consecutive weeks before one or two missed days. Before the hypnotherapy, R. was missing one to two days per week. His mother reported an obvious shift in his attitude about being better able to do things other children could do. Also, his mother reported that she took a trip out of state, something she would not have considered doing before. This behavior followed the indirect suggestion given in the story.

The boy's mother and father had become more active together. She reported that they had begun to leave R. at home with a baby sitter so they could attend social functions. They both felt more free to be with each other and away from their son. Although there were still other marital issues, the couple-system began to restructure itself without revolving around the son. In a nine-month follow-up, the mother reported that these changes had continued throughout the school year and through summer vacation.

In this case study, Ericksonian hypnotherapy was used to intervene in the family system and help reduce symptoms of asthma. Two metaphorical stories were designed to shift the child's attitude from a belief that he was a victim of physical symptoms to a belief that he could maintain more control of bodily processes. The hypnotherapy targeted for change the structure of the family system so that the mother and father functioned more fully as a couple. The interactions with the son became more normalized and the child's symptoms and medications were reduced. After a nine-month follow-up, the change was reported to have been maintained.

Thus, the use of Ericksonian hypnotherapy was a useful modality in accomplishing treatment goals. Since this case study cannot be generalized to the general population, more research needs to be conducted using Ericksonian hypnotherapy as well as other treatment modalities for chronic illness of all kinds. As Erickson knew, we all have unconscious resources for overcoming life difficulties. These resources may be able to significantly alter psychobiological processes, as well as lead to change in the pattern of family interaction.

References

American Lung Association. (1986). Support Group Meeting for Parents of Asthmatic Children. Houston, TX.

Aronoff, G.M., Aronoff, S., & Peck, L.W. (1975). Hypnotherapy in the treatment of bronchial asthma. *Annals of Allergy, 34,* 356-362.

Barber, T.X. (1984). Changing unchangeable bodily processes by suggestions: A new look at hypnosis, cognitions, imaginings and the mind-body problem. In A.A. Sheikh (Ed.), *Imagination and healing.* Farmingdale, N.Y.: Baywood.

Barbour, J. (1980). Medigrams: Self-hypnosis and asthma. *American Family Physician, 21,* 173.

Collison, D.R. (1975). Which asthmatic patients should be treated by hypnotherapy? *Medical Journal of Australia, 1,* 776-781.

Conners, C. (1983). Psychological management of the asthmatic child. *Clinical Review of Allergy, (1)* 163-177.

Erickson, M. (1983). In E. Rossi, M. Ryan, & F. Sharp (Eds.), *Healing in hypnosis.* New York: Irvington.

Feldman, G.M. (1976). The effect of biofeedback training on respiratory resistance of asthmatic children. *Psychosomatic Medicine, 38,* 27-34.

Gardner, G., & Olness, K. (1981). *Hypnosis and hypnotherapy with children.* Orlando, FL: Grune & Stratton.

Hall, H. (1984). In imagery and cancer. In A.A. Sheikh (Ed.), *Imagination and healing.* Farmingdale, N.Y.: Baywood.

Hoffman, L. (1985). Beyond power and control: Toward a "second order" family systems therapy. *Family Systems Medicine, 3* (4): 381-396.

Hoffman, L. (1986). *Second-order cybernetics and family systems work.* Southwest Regional Practice Institute for Family Services of America, San Antonio, TX.

Kershaw, C. (1979). *Effects of visual imagery and relaxation on the psychophysiology of diabetic functioning.* Unpublished doctoral dissertation, East Texas State University, Commerce, TX.

Khan, A.U. (1977). Effectiveness of biofeedback and counter-conditioning in the treatment of bronchial asthma. *Journal of Psychosomatic Research, 21,* 97-104.

Lankton, S., & Lankton, C. (1983). *The answer within: A clinical framework of Ericksonian hypnotherapy.* New York: Brunner/Mazel.

Lankton, S., & Lankton, C. (1985). *Attitude and family structure protocol* (workshop handout). Ericksonian Approaches to Psychotherapy: Advanced Training. Gulf Breeze, FL.

Lankton S., & Lankton C. (1986). *Ericksonian approaches to psychotherapy: Advanced training.* Gulf Breeze, FL.

Pelletier, K. (1977). *Mind as healer, mind as slayer.* New York: Delta.

Rossi, E. (1986). *The psychobiology of mind-body healing: New concepts of therapeutic hypnosis.* New York: W.W. Norton.

Scherr, M., & Crawford, P. (1978). Three-year evaluation of biofeedback techniques in the treatment of children with chronic asthma in a summer camp environment. *Annals of Allergy, 41,* 288-292.

Watzlawick, P., Beavin, J.H., & Jackson, D.D. (1967). *Pragmatics of human communication: A study of interactional patterns, pathologies and paradoxes.* New York: Norton.
Watzlawick, P., & Weakland, J. (1974). *Change.* New York: W.W. Norton.
Wilkinson, J. (1981). Hypnotherapy in the psychosomatic approach to illness: A review. *Journal of the Royal Society of Medicine, 74* (7), 525-530.

Ericksonian Utilization in Shyness Intervention with Adolescents

Eric R. Aronson, Psy.D. Cand.

The development and treatment of shyness in adolescents were examined from various theoretical perspectives. An Ericksonian approach to adolescent shyness intervention was outlined, including theoretical principles as well as clinical techniques. This brief-therapy approach was utilized in the individual treatment of two shy adolescent males. Results indicated that Ericksonian therapy can be effective in increasing the adolescent's sociability, confidence, and self-esteem and in reducing self-consciousness, anxiety, and isolation, according to self-report and teachers' ratings. The findings are consistent with the conceptualization of Ericksonian shyness intervention as a method of liberating and utilizing the resources of the adolescent's unconscious mind.

The adolescent years, from 12 to 18, are replete with societal demands and expectations. Not only must teenagers adjust to their changing bodies, but they must also cope with pressure to be popular with their peers, and especially with the opposite sex. These pressures place a heavy burden on those adolescents who suffer from shyness.

Address reprint requests to: Eric R. Aronson, School of Professional Psychology, University of Denver, 2300 South Gaylord Street, Denver, CO 80208. Appendices are also available on request.

I gratefully acknowledge the valuable assistance of Yvonne M. Dolan, Evelyn S. Paley, Josiah B. Dodds, and Mark Disorbio in conducting the research and reviewing the manuscript.

Although shyness affects more teenage girls than boys (Zimbardo & Radl, 1981), both girls and boys experience shyness—but in somewhat different ways. For example, girls in our society are often expected to be attractive, whereas boys are more often expected to be assertive. These expectations promote feelings of inadequacy in shy children.

Other sex differences exist that are beyond the scope of this monograph (Glasgow & Arkowitz, 1975; Pilkonis, 1977). However, shyness is generally characterized by particular behavioral, affective, and cognitive components that apply equally to boys and girls. Behaviorally, shy adolescents tend to be loners. The boy who sits alone in the cafeteria, the girl who refrains from going to parties—these are the children who avoid people and social situations (Mitchell & Orr, 1974). They also lack specific social skills and, therefore, do not interact as effectively as their nonshy peers (Curran, 1977). For instance, they may not know how to start a conversation, or ask someone out on a date, or refuse a request. These social skills are often related to assertiveness; thus, the shy adolescent tends to act nonassertively.

In addition to withdrawal, shy persons' nonverbal behavior may reflect timidness or anxiety. Fearful facial expressions, a soft tone of voice, rigid posture, and gestures such as fidgeting comprise the nonverbal communication of the teenager who is shy. Underlying the appearance of anxiety are strong feelings of anxiety. Shy children usually feel nervous or fearful in social situations, and this tends to motivate withdrawal. Similarly, they are easily embarrassed; any encounter with another child (or adult) may be seen as a potentially humiliating experience.

The poor quality of their social interactions sometimes elicits from adolescents feelings of depression and despair. One teenage girl, for example, said she felt "bummed 'cause I'll *never* get along with people." Yet, contrary to popular opinion, shy people do not always have an "I'm Not OK—You're OK" attitude (Harris, 1969). Some may feel an undercurrent of anger and resentment toward others, whom they view as getting their way far more often, or as critical or rejecting (Zimbardo, 1977).

Shy adolescents seem to experience a variety of unrealistic beliefs and expectations (Girodo, 1978) in addition to shy feelings and behaviors. The most common is self-consciousness, or a recurrent sense that one is being negatively evaluated by others (Buss, 1980). For instance, a girl of 17 dreaded her high school prom because she was sure all eyes would be on her and her awkward dancing. Along with her self-consciousness was anticipation of failure; that is, a strong conviction that she would make a fool of herself.

Most teenagers who are shy also have low self-esteem (Zimbardo & Radl, 1981). Their self-image is marred by feelings of inferiority, inadequacy, and unloveability. It is as if they were somehow intrinsically bad or damaged and, therefore, less worthwhile as individuals than their classmates. Thus, shy children's beliefs and attitudes may be both irrational and self-defeating.

Treatment of Shyness: Various Perspectives

Shyness intervention is still clearly in the first timid stages of research. Most clinicians who address this problem focus on a single aspect, such as social anxiety, withdrawal, or self-esteem. Very rarely in the literature does the term *shyness* actually appear. Nevertheless, it is possible to infer, from the components that do get addressed, how various theoretical orientations might conceptualize shyness and its treatment.

For example, an existential approach (Frankl, 1963; Yalom, 1980) might focus on shyness as a world view, or as a way that certain individuals create meaning out of their everyday experiences. The shy adolescent has developed an opinion that the world is dangerous, hostile, and fundamentally hopeless; life seems threatening because of the numerous possibilities for failure and rejection. Thus, existential psychotherapists might encourage shy adolescents to accept responsibility for making themselves unhappy and to seek greater satisfaction in life (Perls, 1969; van Kaam, 1966). They may also encourage them to develop a personal identity that gives them a sense of purpose or meaning, and a sense of hope rather than hopeless isolation (Frankl, 1978).

In contrast, psychoanalytic formulations of shyness tend to focus on relevant psychodynamics and personality structures. Shyness may involve developmental "fixations" (Freud, 1953), or deviations from normal separation-individuation (Mahler, 1968), or identity-formation (Erikson, 1963, 1968). Many shy adolescents are actually diagnosed as suffering from an "identity disorder" (American Psychiatric Association, 1980). Perhaps shyness is related to an inadequately functioning ego, or to an early childhood disorder of the self (Kohut, 1971). Or it may represent a withdrawing interpersonal style (Horney, 1945).

Whether the shy adolescent is experiencing low self-esteem, inadequate object relations, or an identity crisis, psychoanalytic treatment typically consists of free associations about the past, as well as working through conflicts and transference feelings toward the therapist (Aichhorn, 1983). Although many adolescents may not take well to the analyst's couch, most are able to talk about themselves well enough to engage in the psychoanalytic process.

Whereas the existential perspective on shyness emphasizes individuals' awareness and world view and the psychodynamic perspective emphasizes ego development, a cognitive-behavioral perspective would emphasize learning history, such as the reinforcement of a child's poor self-image by classmates and bullies. A specific assessment instrument might be selected in order to determine which shy behaviors are to be modified (Dowrick & Gilligan, 1985).

The behavior therapist may view shyness as a social phobia. In order to extinguish conditioned anxiety and social avoidance, shy adolescents may be treated with systematic or in-vivo desensitization, as in fantasy or practice dating (Arkowitz, 1977; Arkowitz, Hinton, Perl, & Himadi, 1978; Christensen & Arkowitz, 1974; Christensen, Arkowitz, & Anderson, 1975; Curran, 1975; Curran & Gilbert, 1975; Martinson & Zerface, 1970; Mitchell & Orr, 1974; O'Brien & Borkovec, 1977).

Alternative cognitive-behavioral treatment strategies include reducing shy children's learned helplessness (Seligman, 1975); providing training in assertiveness and social skills (Fischetti, Curran, & Wessberg, 1977; Twentyman & McFall, 1975); modeling social interaction (O'Connor, 1969); and challenging unrealistic beliefs and expectations (Buss, 1980; Glass, Gottman, & Smurak, 1976). An approach that combines cognitive and behavioral interventions may be especially effective with shy adolescents (Girodo, 1978; Zimbardo, 1977; Zimbardo & Radl, 1981).

Shyness exists in families as well as in individuals, and various types of family therapy have been employed with the families of shy adolescents. One approach (Minuchin, 1974) attempts to alter the family structure by clarifying boundaries and manipulating alliances within the family. Another (Satir, 1967) aims at improving family communication. Haley (1976) and Madanes (1981) utilize strategic interventions such as detailed explanations or homework assignments in order to solve the family's central problem (shyness). All three approaches try to enable the family system to function smoothly without the symptom of shyness.

Ericksonian Utilization

Theory and Rationale

Ericksonian hypnotherapy offers a number of distinct advantages in the treatment of shy adolescents. It is a naturalistic approach, utilizes unconscious resources, is client-centered, and relies on cooperation and trust. It is also ego-supportive, conveys a sense of choice, makes use of resistance, and is useful in brief therapy.

Just as the above-mentioned perspectives on shyness intervention are based on a coherent system of theory and practice, so is the Ericksonian perspective. In fact, that perspective draws its construct validity from precedents set by traditional hypnosis. For example, hypnosis has been used with adults in order to increase assertiveness (de Voge, 1977); to increase self-confidence or sense of mastery (Brown & Chaves, 1980; Bruhn, 1983; Gardner, 1976; Wollman, 1978); to increase self-esteem or improve self-concept (de Voge, 1977; Grant, 1982; Howard, 1979; Hylland, 1976; Wagenfeld & Carlson, 1979); and to reduce anxiety (Grant, 1982; Howard, 1979). Similarly, with children and adolescents, hypnosis has been used to increase self-confidence or a sense of mastery (Oldridge, 1982); to increase self-esteem or improve self-concept (Fung & Lazar, 1983; Johnson, Johnson, Olson, & Newman, 1981; Koe, 1982; Russell, 1984); and to reduce anxiety (Fung & Lazar, 1983; Oldridge, 1982; Russell, 1984).

In contrast to formal approaches to hypnosis in which clients are "placed in a trance," Ericksonian hypnosis is a more indirect, conversational approach based on utilizing and potentiating the resources of the unconscious mind (Gilligan, 1982). Ericksonian utilization is the process of incorporating clients' ongoing behaviors and perceptions into the therapeutic change process (Dolan, 1985). Since it involves utilizing that which clients present, this treatment approach has been described as a naturalistic one. That is, rather than engaging people in activities and situations that are alien and contrived, Ericksonian hypnosis seeks to enter their world and enable them to find solutions with their own internal maps (Lankton & Lankton, 1983).

For example, families often inadvertently perform or undergo certain characteristic inductions automatically in their everyday interactions, without the conscious awareness of individual family members (Ritterman, 1983; Lankton & Lankton, 1986). The shy adolescent in the family, it might be said, is inadvertently hypnotized to stay out of family discussions, and other members may be hypnotized to keep him or her out of the discussion. Through Ericksonian methods, this naturally occurring induction may be utilized by the therapist to ensure that adolescents will listen to a particular discussion, or for other clinical purposes.

Ericksonian therapists assume that individuals have within their unconscious minds the resources to utilize for change (Dolan, 1985). This is especially important with shy children, since they may present as helpless and nonassertive; they are not likely to volunteer the solutions to their problems. Thus, therapists must look for answers in the messages they convey indirectly, through a veil of symbolism and metaphor, and they must respect all those messages (Lankton & Lankton, 1983).

Ericksonian utilization is, therefore, a process "of evoking and utilizing a patient's own mental processes in ways that are outside his [sic] usual range of intentional or voluntary control" (Erickson, Rossi, & Rossi, 1976,

p. 19). This process also involves respect for the integrity of the individual (Dolan, 1985). Rather than telling clients what to do in therapy or what language to speak, as in some treatment approaches, Ericksonian psychotherapy strives to let clients plan their own menu for treatment (Erickson & Rossi, 1979). Shy adolescents, who may feel threatened by a more structured and authoritarian approach, are likely to feel more comfortable and secure with an Ericksonian one.

Whereas some treatment approaches (such as the cognitive-behavioral approach) focus on clients' behavior to the exclusion of the therapist's, the Ericksonian approach emphasizes the client-therapist relationship—not in the classical sense of transference and countertransference, but rather in a spirit of cooperation and trust. It is as if therapist and client were co-conspirators in a plot to discover new growth and fulfillment.

Nowhere is this co-conspiratorial attitude more apparent than in the Ericksonian hypnotherapist's response to client resistance. Rather than seeking to avoid resistance or interpret it in the hope that it will be "worked-through," the hypnotherapist attempts to utilize resistance and accept it as a valid form of comunication (Lankton & Lankton, 1983).

For example, a 16-year-old boy seen in family therapy came out from under his shell of shyness and demanded attention whenever his parents argued during a session. "You don't care about me," he whined, as the tears streamed down his face. The parents inevitably abandoned their argument in order to comfort their son. The therapist did not denounce this behavior as a form of manipulation, but instead complimented the boy in a meaningful tone of voice about how effectively he protected his parents from conflict. Whether this is viewed as a paradoxical intervention (Selvini Palazzoli, Cecchin, Prata, & Boscolo, 1978; Weeks & L'Abate, 1982) or simply as communicating acceptance of the client in an undeniable way (Dolan, 1985), positively reframing the adolescent's behavior made use of what could otherwise have been considered resistance.

Along with utilization, Ericksonian psychotherapy works by a process of indirect suggestion. The underlying message is: "If you come to me for help in changing your behavior, chances are you desire to do it for yourself and you'll work out some clever excuses for not changing if I tell you directly how to change. Yet, if I tell your unconscious mind how to change, in language you understand on a symbolic level, and, if I ultimately leave the decision how to change up to you, it is more likely that you will actually opt for change."

Thus, Ericksonian practitioners teach choice (Lankton & Lankton, 1983)—choice in how to change, when to change, and what meaning to make of that change. When therapists try to dictate the terms of change to adolescents, the typical response is a digging in of heels and a rebellious "Make me!", either aggressively stated or, in the case of shy teenagers, passive-aggressively implied.

Ericksonian psychotherapists tend to be hypnotists, since communication to the unconscious mind is hypnotic communication, whatever form it takes. Yet the kind of hypnosis they practice is not the authoritarian "You will levitate your hand" variety; it is the variety that teaches choice. "You may choose to" can be a common phrase in Ericksonian work. Therefore, the Ericksonian approach is not only an effective strategy in working with shy adolescents, but it is also a humanistic one in that it respects the freedom and integrity of each client. The client's unconscious mind can operate autonomously and intelligently (Erickson, 1985); therefore, it deserves the therapist's acknowledgement and respect.

The Ericksonian orientation is also an ego-supportive one. That is, it is growth-oriented and strives to facilitate the development of a sense of self-determination and mastery. The nurturance of the self, the indomitable human spirit, and all its capabilities are at the center of Ericksonian intervention.

Through communicating acceptance to clients, both verbally and non-verbally, Ericksonian therapists generate the "yes" set of agreement or sense of hope that makes change possible (Dolan, 1985). This process is crucial to the treatment of shy adolescents, whose sense of self-worth is meager at best. In an environment of nurturing acceptance, they can begin to develop enough self-confidence and trust to utilize the resources of their unconscious mind. In a supportive world, they can begin to unlock the gates that their conscious mind has erected, and thereby lead themselves along the path toward actualization.

In summary, Ericksonian hypnotherapy is based on the concepts of utilization, cooperation, indirect suggestion, choice, and undeniable acceptance—all advantages in the treatment of shy adolescents. An additional advantage is that it is a particularly effective approach to brief therapy. Adolescents enter treatment through referral by parents, by schools, and by the courts. Very rarely do they seek treatment voluntarily for themselves. This is even more true of shy teens, who feel stigmatized by the very idea of counseling. Talking about yourself to an adult for an hour? Most adolescents would sooner be tarred and feathered.

In situations whose parameters are not defined by self-referral and private practice, long-term therapy is often unrealistic or impractical. Typically, shy adolescents are treated by overworked school counselors, or by caseworkers in hospital or mental health centers with large caseloads. In these cases, short-term therapy is the only feasible alternative. Yet, within a period of a few weeks, Ericksonian psychotherapists can frequently facilitate significant improvement in adolescents' self-images, assertiveness, emotional comfort, and social behavior. When conscious barriers are circumvented and unconscious potentials are utilized, adolescents who are timid and anxious may quickly find hidden reserves of comfort and security, confidence, and growth.

Stages of Treatment and Corresponding Techniques

Ericksonian hypnotherapy is built on a foundation of acceptance; three major treatment stages are its basic building blocks. These stages consist of joining and establishing rapport, utilization and indirect suggestion, and reorientation and integration (Dolan, 1985). Each stage may be considered separately, along with its corresponding therapeutic techniques— although all are in some ways interrelated.

Joining and rapport form the cornerstore of the Ericksonian approach, since that approach is built on cooperation and trust. Ericksonian therapists attempt to meet clients at their model of the world (Lankton & Lankton, 1983); that is, to express an understanding and acceptance of clients' attitudes and beliefs. When clients observe that therapists are "with them," they are likely to become more comfortable and relaxed.

The most fundamental method of establishing rapport is through casual conversation (Dolan, 1985). The therapist talks to the client about his or her interests and activities, about the problem as he or she defines it, and about what life will be like after the problem is solved. Other important topics include exceptions to the problem and areas of success in the client's life (de Shazer, 1985). Asking these questions in a meaningful tone of voice may facilitate a conversational induction (Erickson et al., 1976), in which the client begins to focus on the positive and on possibilities for change.

During the conversation, it is important for the therapist to convey to clients an understanding and acceptance of what they are saying. So, for example, if a shy teenager is talking about how important his dead spider collection is to him, it is essential that the therapist acknowledge that, regardless of his or her own feelings about collecting dead spiders. Through verbal and nonverbal communication, Ericksonian therapists convey acceptance of their clients in an undeniable way (Dolan, 1985).

One of the most powerful techniques for conveying acceptance and establishing rapport is that of pacing (Bandler & Grinder, 1979). Pacing consists of carefully observing clients' behavior and then reflecting that behavior or a portion of the behavior back to them. Verbal pacing refers to talking the same "language" as a client; that is, using the same or similar words, phrases, and grammatical structure. So, as a therapist with shy adolescents, I find myself repeating phrases such as "Y' know" and "Yeah, what a drag."

In addition, I often try to use language that emphasizes the same sensory modality (auditory, visual, kinesthetic) as my client's language (Bandler & Grinder, 1979). If a client says "I see" and "It looks as if," I will not respond by saying "It sounds like" or "I get the feeling"; rather, I will mirror back the same sensory modality that my client prefers.

Nonverbal pacing is equally important. This consists of observing and reflecting individual clients' voice tone and volume, rhythm of speech, body posture, facial expressions, gestures, and other elements of nonverbal communication (Dolan, 1985). I may reflect these back to my client either directly or indirectly, as in varying my speech rate or hand movements in time with a client's breathing. This latter form of pacing is known as partial indirect mirroring (Dolan, 1985) or crossover mirroring (Bandler & Grinder, 1979). The advantage of this and other types of pacing is that it conveys to clients a sense of commonality and understanding, which in turn can foster feelings of relaxation, comfort, and security. For shy children, relaxation is an essential first step toward overcoming social anxiety.

Once rapport has been established, therapists can then go on to do the actual work of therapy: building confidence, facilitating new responses and attitudes, and so forth. However, it is noteworthy that the task of pacing and joining clients does not end until the therapy has ended. Interventions will not be effective unless they are embedded in an overall pattern of understanding, acceptance, and rapport (Dolan, 1985).

Ericksonian hypnotherapists use a variety of intervention techniques and strategies depending upon the individual case (Erickson et al., 1976). Three that are particularly relevant to shyness intervention with adolescents are reframing symptoms and presenting problems (Erickson, 1985), dissociating from anxiety and associating to relaxation by means of associational cues (Erickson & Rossi, 1979; Erickson et al., 1976), and activating resources of the unconscious mind through the use of metaphor (Dolan, 1985; Lankton & Lankton, 1983).

These intervention techniques are especially applicable to many shy adolescents because they address the resistance that can be so frustrating to therapists at times. In therapy, shy adolescents express their resistance to treatment either by silence or passive-aggressive behavior, or occasionally by open hostility. Ericksonian methods of indirect suggestion head off such resistance by accepting it and utilizing it therapeutically. Just as pacing is central to establishing rapport, so are strategies of indirect suggestion or leading (Bandler & Grinder, 1979) central to bypassing conscious barriers and leading clients toward new learning.

Reframing (Erickson, 1985) is perhaps the most basic form of utilization, as well as a most potent method of shyness intervention. Reframing refers to ascribing new meanings to symptomatic behavior (de Shazer, 1985) or redefining a problem and changing its function so that it may serve as a therapeutic resource (Watzlawick, Weakland, & Fisch, 1974).

An example of reframing in shyness intervention concerns a 15-year-old girl who is so self-conscious that she never raises her hand to speak in class. Rather than confronting her for her lack of assertiveness, the therapist compliments her on being "tranquil" and "unassuming," and possessing a certain "quiet wisdom." Unlike the behavioral technique that attempts to prolong anxiety in order to extinguish avoidance behavior (Curran et al., 1976), this reframing technique attempts to extinguish anxiety about being shy—an essential first step toward learning nonshy behaviors.

Just as these reframes help reduce anxiety and facilitate relaxation in shy children, so can certain techniques of association and dissociation. Since social anxiety constitutes a large portion of shyness, it follows that therapists help their clients to dissociate from or stop focusing on what makes them anxious. People can gain some distance from anxiety-provoking situations by imagining they are watching them on television, on a movie screen, reflected in a car window, and so forth (Lankton & Lankton, 1983). When an uncomfortable situation (such as speaking in front of a full classroom) no longer seems so immediate, people tend to feel less anxious or shy.

Along with techniques for dissociating from anxiety, it is helpful to educate children on ways to associate to feelings of relaxation and comfort (Dolan, 1985). This may be done by means of associational cues, or stimuli that elicit particular unconscious responses (Erickson & Rossi, 1979; Erickson et al., 1976).

With shy adolescents, it is often important to find out which situations and accompanying sensory experiences (feelings, sights, sounds) stimulate a sense of comfort and security. One may ask directly, but this may provoke the same type of resistance as formally stating, "Now I am going to hypnotize you." Adolescents easily feel threatened by any perceived loss of control, and it is usually best to avoid using the word "hypnosis" altogether; hence, the emphasis on a naturalistic approach.

Often an effective way to elicit associational cues for relaxation and comfort in adolescents is to ask about favorite interests and activities, especially those enjoyed "by yourself" in a "peaceful and quiet place." Associated sights, sounds, and feelings should be explored. Therapists may determine which of these are the most effective by observing clients' relaxation responses whenever these subjects are spoken about. It is especially important for therapists to be relaxed when eliciting and then utilizing these associations (Dolan, 1985).

Once appropriate associational cues have been established, therapists may help clients to integrate those cues into their everyday experiences so that they can be accessed in anxiety-provoking situations. For example: "When you give that speech / take that test / go on that date, you can think about the wonderfully relaxing feeling of camping out under the stars, with a gentle breeze blowing," and so on.

Reframing may also be utilized in the integration of associational cues (Dolan, 1985). For instance, in the case of the aforementioned 15-year-old girl: "As you're sitting there, with your arms crossed and your eyes directed at the floor (pacing), you can really get in touch with that quiet wisdom of yours. And you can also enjoy that relaxing, comforting feeling as you think those same thoughts when you are called on to answer a question in class."

In addition to reframing and associational cues, the use of metaphors can greatly enhance the effectiveness of shyness intervention (Lankton & Lankton, 1983). A metaphor is a story or anecdote that facilitates unconscious learning through symbolic communication. It may be a proverb, a fairy tale, a story made up by the therapist, or a personal anecdote about a friend or acquaintance, as Milton H. Erickson was so fond of telling (Haley, 1973; Rosen, 1982).

One approach is formulating a therapeutic metaphor to be isomorphic to the unique situation; that is, it should fit each client's life situation and view of the world. A good test of this is whether or not clients become interested and absorbed in the story. In these instances it contains the following elements: the client's current problem, what he or she wants to attain in therapy, resistance to change, incentive to change (or fear of not changing), an unanticipated therapeutic resource (such as an associational cue for relaxation or confidence), attainment of the desired outcome, and predictable temporary regression to the problem state that eventually leads to further change (Dolan, 1985).

Using this format, it is possible to construct a metaphor for a shy adolescent that resembles the following outline: A teenage boy or girl is unhappy because he or she is shy (self-conscious, inhibited, anxious in social situations). The child is really looking forward to the day when he or she will be self-confident (popular, assertive). Of course, the child is afraid that he or she will always be shy because of some formidable obstacle or personality trait, or that overcoming shyness would mean giving up something valuable. However, remaining shy poses one of the child's worst fears. Then, he or she discovers something (a magic key, a favorite place, a special friend) that is instrumental in starting to become less shy. Sufficient detail can be elaborated to teach how he or she comes to and does enjoy the wonderful feeling of being the kind of person he or she wants to be. And although there are still occasional periods of feeling shy, it is at those times that the person realizes what new resources he or she has acquired for coping with shyness.

Again, it is important that this type of metaphor be isomorphic. Whether the story begins with "You know, that reminds me of . . . ," "My friend John . . . ," or "Once upon a time . . . ," it should be custom-tailored to fit the individual client; that is, details of the story may match or symbolize personally meaningful elements of the client's life.

Symbolism is especially effective in working with shy adolescents. Teenagers tend to squirm anxiously when adults talk about their problems (and shyness is no exception). Yet they usually feel less threatened by stories about the fear of someone climbing a mountain for the first time, or the self-consciousness of the emperor with his new clothes. Fables, novels, movies, plays, and, above all, personal experiences—these provide a wealth of images from which the creative therapist can draw in constructing a metaphor to fit a particular client with a particular problem.

In review, the typical treatment strategies in Ericksonian shyness intervention may often include joining or establishing rapport with the client (through casual conversation, pacing, and communicating acceptance in an undeniable way) and bypassing conscious blocks to utilize the resources of the unconscious mind through various techniques of leading or indirect suggestion (including reframing problems, dissociation from anxiety, associational cues for comfort and security, and isomorphic metaphors).

However, there remains a third stage of intervention that is critically important in treating shy adolescents—that of reorientation to the here-and-now with appropriate integration of new learning. In other words, Ericksonian hypnotherapists try not to leave their clients "hanging" at the end of an illuminating therapy session, but instead try to maximize the possibility that the client will continue to make progress after the session.

In order to accomplish this, it is important to protect the conscious mind from learnings for which it is not yet ready, and to protect unconscious learnings from the curiosity and possible intrusiveness of the conscious mind. Therefore, the therapist may wish to suggest amnesia for what was learned hypnotically during the therapy session.

There are a number of ways to induce therapeutic amnesia. Indirectly, the therapist may return to the topic of casual conversation that preceded the hypnotic learning. Or the therapist may use a pattern interruption (such as a joke, a pun, or a puzzling question) in order to distract the conscious mind (Erickson, 1985; Gilligan, 1982).

Amnesia may be induced directly by telling clients, "You will only remember what you wish to remember." In the words of Erickson (1985), "I want you to understand consciously whatever you need to; I want you to understand unconsciously whatever you need to" (p. 126). Or the therapist may use an approach that combines direct and indirect (distraction) strategies: "And you can forget to remember and remember to forget" (C. E. Johnson, personal communication, February 23, 1985). The suggestion of choice conveys the therapist's respect for clients' unconscious wisdom about what to remember and what to therapeutically "forget" (Lankton & Lankton, 1983). This sense of trust, along with the protection hypnotic amnesia affords, may make the difference between a shy adolescent's staying in treatment or terminating prematurely.

Other techniques may be helpful in integrating therapeutic learnings. Clients often feel the "force of closure" at the end of a session of hypnosis, as at the end of treatment (Lankton & Lankton, 1983). At these times, when a strong need for integration is experienced, it is beneficial to orient clients toward the future with a suggestion that they will further integrate all that has been learned, or at least as much as the unconscious mind deems appropriate.

By a process of future-pacing (Grinder & Bandler, 1981), clients may be guided toward integration and actualization of their potentials. One need only ask clients to imagine themselves in the future, after they have attained the changes they seek, and to experience that future in as much sensory detail as possible.

Thus, adolescents may be encouraged to think about and describe the sights, sounds, and feelings of being self-confident, popular, socially adept, and pleased with themselves. They may also be asked to look back at the intermediate steps they took that helped them reach their desired outcome.

It is especially important in orienting shy adolescents toward the future to use positive and unquestioning language. Adolescents tend to be doubtful and often cynical about the future, and those who are shy are even more pessimistic. Therefore, therapists are wise to use the technique of presupposition (Dolan, 1985), also known as creating a time bind (Erickson et al., 1976) or anticipating change in order to facilitate it (Haley, 1973).

When therapists employ presupposition, they assume that the client is (definitely) going to achieve a desired change. So, rather than asking,

"What would it be like for you if you were less shy?", one may ask, "What will it be like when you have become quite confident in yourself?" Adding reframes and associational cues, one might suggest, "And you can wonder (choice) how wonderful it will feel to go fishing / walk along the beach / and so forth (associational cues for relaxation) when you have graduated from high school (presupposition) and learned to use that quiet wisdom of yours (reframe of problem) to gain the support and admiration of some very special friends (future-pacing with presuppositions)."

An essential part of future orientation in helping clients to integrate what they have learned is the prediction of a relapse (Haley, 1973). In other words, therapists predict that, either during treatment or following termination, clients will reexperience some of the symptoms that brought them into treatment. However, it is important to frame such predictions in a way that also facilitates further change, that is, by predicting temporary regressions leading to new learning and growth (Dolan, 1985).

An example of this type of prediction is Erickson's statement: I want you to go back and feel as badly as you did when you first came in with the problem, because I want you to see if there is anything from that time that you wish to recover and salvage. (Haley, 1973, p. 31)

An alternative approach is that discussed in relation to metaphors: "You will occasionally feel shy again, and at those times you will remember the ways you have learned to feel good about yourself."

Besides enhancing the desired therapeutic outcome and thereby making change more permanent (Dolan, 1985), predicting a relapse may function paradoxically to increase clients' motivation to change (Weeks & L'Abate, 1982). The prediction places perceived control of regression in the hands of the therapist and challenges adolescents to utilize their rebellious or passive-aggressive tendencies in order to continue to change. However, one should bear in mind that predicting a relapse without framing it appropriately (connecting it to further growth) may contradict positive future-pacing and presupposition of change.

These techniques of shyness intervention reflect the basic principles of Ericksonian treatment: joining clients in their world of experience, and helping clients to integrate what they have learned in ways that further facilitate personal growth. It is possible to combine these into a cohesive, general treatment package for shy adolescents. It must be noted that Ericksonian therapy is client-centered. Therefore, when using a general outline, treatment should be structured around the needs and resources of the individual client. For what is utilization if not a single flower's prescription for blooming?

Case Histories

Case One

Kurt, a 13-year-old male, attended public school in a rural western town. He was referred to a clinical psychology intern at the school for individual therapy. His presenting problems included low self-esteem, poor social skills, and lack of academic motivation.

At the time of referral, Kurt was a shy and withdrawn seventh-grader. He had no friends and could not identify anything positive about himself or his life. When he did interact with classmates, he often provoked fights or was teased by other children. Kurt did not speak up in class, nor did he ask teachers for help. His schoolwork was especially poor; he showed little interest in any of his classes and his grades were extremely low.

Kurt's home environment was quite stressful. His father, who worked in plumbing and carpentry, frequently quarreled with him and was reported to be physically abusive. His mother, a housewife, seemed somewhat distant and ineffectual. Kurt was given numerous family responsibilities, including caring for a younger sister and preparing his father's breakfast at 4:00 a.m. He got little sleep.

This adolescent was seen in school for six weekly treatment sessions. Treatment utilized an Ericksonian approach and followed the general outline of a structured clinical treatment package. Joining and pacing were employed in order to establish rapport, with an emphasis on conveying acceptance in an undeniable way. Presenting problems were explored and reframed. Associational cues for relaxation were identified and strengthened along with dissociation from anxiety.

Three metaphors or stories were told to Kurt, which symbolically addressed his problems and utilized his unconscious resources and strengths. The first was the Greek myth about the 12 tasks of Hercules (Hamilton, 1969); this acknowledged Kurt's extraordinary responsibilities, as well as his inner strength and courage. The second metaphor was the story of how the legendary Arthur drew the sword from the anvil and was thus declared the rightful king of England (Pyle, 1903). This symbolized Kurt's struggle to develop self-confidence, assert himself, and realize his leadership potential.

The third metaphor was written and mailed to Kurt at home, since he was absent from school the week after the fifth session. His therapist wrote a story that addressed his shyness, associational cues for comfort and security, and the goal of functioning in a nonshy manner.

The final therapy session focused on positive future-pacing, along with integration of new learnings (including associational cues) whenever he felt anxious or unsure of himself. He revealed that he had taken a strong interest in creative writing, one of his classes in school, and that he hoped to publish some of the stories he had written.

At the end of treatment, Kurt described himself as "a good kid," "hard-working," and "pretty creative." He predicted that the following school year would find him "more in charge" of his life, popular in school, and proud of his achievements in creative writing. At this time (the end of the school year), he had already made some friends and started to improve his grades.

Two of Kurt's teachers were given a questionnaire before and after treatment that inquired about the weekly frequency of observed behaviors related to shyness. (Those behaviors were embedded among other behaviors.) Both teachers reported a marked decrease in social anxiety or awkwardness (50%), anxiety about school performance (40-50%), fights with peers (40-50%), self-consciousness or embarrassment (40-90%), negative statements about himself (50-80%), anticipating failure (66-80%), and withdrawal or isolating himself (80-100%).

Behaviors that increased with treatment included smiling (100%), being helpful to teachers (100%), and being cheerful and friendly (100-166%). Although these ratings are subjective in nature, the data lend support to the hypothesis that Ericksonian hypnosis may be helpful in the alleviation of shyness in adolescents.

Case Two

Jim is a 13-year-old male who also attended a rural public school in the western United States. He was referred for individual therapy with the school psychology intern because of low self-esteem, inadequate social skills, poor academic motivation, and anxiety over social interaction and academic performance.

At the time of referral, the client was described by teachers as a "loner" who was exceptionally quiet and withdrawn in school. He had very few friends and appeared especially anxious in social situations. He also exhibited anxiety over homework and tests. His attendance record was poor and he frequently spent time in the school nurse's office because of physical complaints.

Jim was reported to speak negatively of himself; he did not recognize his personal strengths. According to teachers, those strengths included an outstanding vocabulary, good manners and consideration of others, and exceptional athletic abilities.

Jim's home environment was a lonely one. He lived alone with his mother, a school bus driver who was reportedly depressed and spent little time with him. His father had committed suicide when Jim was less than two years old. An older brother was in the military and had been away from home for a year.

Treatment followed an Ericksonian approach, and the general outline of a clinical treatment package for shy adolescents. In the first session, Jim acted in a hostile and "resistant" manner; he repeatedly insulted the therapist with a long string of obscenities. He insisted that he did not need counseling and said, "I've been in counseling all my life, and I haven't gotten a thing out of it."

In subsequent sessions, Jim became less hostile and talked about his interests and activities. He disclosed that he enjoyed gymnastics, football, soccer, lacrosse, karate, and riding motorcycles. He talked about his ambition some day to be a wealthy lawyer, to live in southern California, and to own "six Lamborghinis, a Cadillac limousine, and a private jet."

During therapy sessions Jim avoided eye contact, talked in a low voice, used a cynical tone, and frequently fidgeted and held his hands in a fist. He also leaned back in his chair and addressed his comments to the wall behind the therapist. The therapist paced these behaviors and interspersed leads for comfort and safety. (For example: "That's right, it really is OK to talk in here.")

Jim revealed that certain popular music served as an associational cue for relaxation and comfort. "When I listen to it," he said, "it takes my mind off things (dissociation); it helps me to kick back and take it easy." He also indicated that upbeat music and thinking about riding a motorcycle served as associational cues for a sense of mastery and self-confidence.

Positive reframing was an integral part of Jim's treatment. For example, when he was hostile or cynical, the therapist praised him on his "good critical eye," and even teased him back in a friendly, good-natured manner, in order to convey acceptance in an undeniable way. Reframes also utilized his associational cues; for instance, his lack of attention was defined as letting himself "kick back and take it easy."

Special attention was given to helping Jim integrate his associational cues for relaxation and confidence into his daily life in relation to his shyness. He was reminded that, when taking a test or in a social situation, he could think about listening to his favorite music or riding a motorcycle. (Since Jim preferred the use of auditory imagery, this was described with an emphasis on details such as "the sound of the wind as you ride.")

Jim's associational cues were further utilized during the course of treatment. For example, the therapist told him a true anecdote (metaphor) about a friend who found that thinking about his motorcycle enabled him to tolerate tedious classes and anxiety-provoking social situations. Future-pacing in the last session included looking ahead to when Jim might be the master of his own life. The therapist predicted times when Jim "might not feel like a master" (relapses), and at those times he could find comfort and self-confidence (further growth) in thinking about listening to music or riding a motorcycle.

According to Jim's teachers, he seemed to be somewhat less shy after short-term therapy. Although one of the two teachers who completed a questionnaire did not quantify her responses beyond "some" or "a lot," one or both of them saw a decrease in the following behaviors: social anxiety or awkwardness, low speaking voice, withdrawal or isolating himself, avoiding eye contact, interacting passively or timidly, anticipating failure, immature or childish behavior, and appearing depressed.

Nonshy behaviors in which teachers reported increases included positive statements about himself and asserting himself appropriately. In general, these changes were not reported for "control" subjects (shy students not seen in treatment) by the above teachers or the teachers surveyed in Case One.

It is interesting to note that teachers reported slight increases in some nonshy behaviors consistent with Jim's hostility and anger, such as cussing, fighting, and talking back to teachers. Although his family background may provide an explanation for his intense anger (as expressed to the therapist in the first session), the results suggest that as he became less shy, in therapy Jim may have also become less reserved about expressing his angry feelings.

During the course of treatment, Jim made several friends, improved his attendance record, and began to show increased academic motivation. More important, he displayed significant improvements in self-esteem, social functioning, and assertiveness, as well as reduced anxiety in test-taking and social situations. Although the results of brief therapy are necessarily limited, the cases of Kurt and Jim illustrate the value of Ericksonian techniques in adolescent shyness intervention.

Discussion

Clearly, there are a variety of approaches to the treatment of shy adolescents. Shyness as a form of psychopathology or personal discomfort consists of a characteristic assortment of symptoms. Specific behavioral, affective, and cognitive components have been identified. The existential, psychodynamic, cognitive-behavioral, and family systems perspectives offer theoretical interpretations and treatment strategies for shy adolescents with varying emphasis placed on individual components. A perspective that differs markedly from these is Ericksonian hypnosis, which is derived from the psychiatric formulations of Milton H. Erickson.

Whereas the existential approach strives to facilitate responsibility and awareness of the adolescent's experience or world view, the Ericksonian approach strives to liberate and utilize resources that reside within the adolescent's unconscious mind. Whereas the psychodynamic approach is primarily a long-term treatment method that emphasizes insight into archaic conflicts and defense mechanisms, the Ericksonian approach is short-term and emphasizes experiential change through indirect suggestion. Whereas the cognitive-behavioral approach downplays the importance of the therapeutic relationship, the Ericksonian approach centers around client-therapist interaction within a context of pacing and undeniable acceptance. Whereas the family systems approach strengthens the functioning of families, the Ericksonian approach may choose to primarily strengthen the resources of the individual shy adolescent family member.

Since adolescents who are shy and reserved in their social interactions are likely to be the same in psychotherapy, these clients require a special treatment strategy that addresses their individual needs. Ericksonian hypnotherapy provides such a strategy. It must be remembered to treat each case as a unique individual, but this paper has concentrated upon a particularly successful pattern of treatment. From joining the adolescent and establishing rapport, through utilization and indirect suggestion, to integration of new learnings into everyday life, the shy youngster may be guided sensitively and empathically toward a more positive self-image, more rewarding relationships, and a brighter outlook on life.

Ericksonian therapists have amassed some effective techniques for the treatment of shy adolescents, including pacing, reframing, dissociation and use of associational cues, metaphors, and future-pacing. Yet there remain several unanswered questions concerning these techniques. Which techniques are most effective in treating specific components of shyness? What additional techniques should be considered in clinical work with shy adolescents? How could the above approach be modified for application to other populations, such as shy children, college students, or adults? Additional research should provide some answers to these questions.

For many teenagers, shyness is a crippling and even devastating affliction. Its consequences are lives spent in isolation and fear. Perhaps the meek shall inherit the earth; in the meantime, Ericksonian interventions are effective means of helping shy adolescents to lead happier and more fulfilling lives.

References

Aichhorn, A. (1983). The transference. In A.H. Esman (Ed.), *The psychiatric treatment of adolescents* (pp. 5-26). New York: International Universities Press.

American Psychiatric Association (1980). *Diagnostic and statistical manual of mental disorders* (3rd ed.). Washington, DC: Author.

Arkowitz, H. (1977). Measurement and modification of minimal dating behavior. In M. Hersen, R.M. Eisler, & P. M. Miller (Eds.), *Progress in behavior modification* (Vol. 5). New York: Academic Press.

Arkowitz, H., Hinton, R., Perl, J., & Himadi, W. (1978). Treatment strategies for dating anxiety in college men based on real-life practice. *The Counseling Psychologist, 4* 41-46.

Bandler, R., & Grinder, J. (1979). *Frogs into princes: Neurolinguistic programming.* Moab, UT: Real People Press.

Brown, J.M., & Chaves, J.F. (1980). Hypnosis in the treatment of sexual dysfunction. *Journal of Sex and Marital Therapy, 6,* 63-64.

Bruhn, R.A. (1983). Effects on hypnosis on counselor trainee skill acquisition and self-perceived confidence (Doctoral dissertation, East Texas State University, 1983). *Dissertation Abstracts International, 43,* 3509A.

Buss, A.H. (1980). *Self-consciousness and social anxiety.* San Francisco: W. H. Freeman.

Christensen, A., & Arkowitz, H. (1974). Preliminary report on practice dating and feedback as treatment for college dating problems. *Journal of Counseling Psychology, 21,* 92-95.

Christensen, A., Arkowitz, H., & Anderson, J. (1975). Practice dating as treatment for college dating inhibitions. *Behaviour Research and Therapy, 13,* 321-331.

Curran, J.P. (1975). Social skills training and systematic desensitization in reducing dating anxiety. *Behaviour Research and Therapy, 13,* 65-68.

Curran, J.P. (1977). Skills training as an approach to the treatment of heterosexual social anxiety: A review. *Psychological Bulletin, 84,* 140-157.

Curran, J.P., & Gilbert, F. S. (1975). A test of the relative effectiveness of a systematic desensitization program and an interpersonal skills training program with date anxious subjects. *Behavior Therapy, 6,* 510-521.

Curran, J.P., Gilbert, F.S., & Little, L.M. (1976). A comparison between behavioral replication training and sensitivity training approaches to heterosexual dating anxiety. *Journal of Counseling Psychology, 23,* 190-196.

de Shazer, S. (1985). *Keys to solution in brief therapy.* New York: W. W. Norton.

de Voge, S. (1977). Use of hypnosis for assertive training and self-concept change in women: A case study. *American Journal of Clinical Hypnosis, 19,* 226-230.

Dolan, Y.M. (1985). *A path with a heart: Ericksonian utilization with resistant and chronic clients.* New York: Brunner/Mazel.

Dowrick, P. W., & Gilligan, C. A. (1985). Social skills and children: An annotated bibliography. *The Behavior Therapist, 10,* 211-213.

Erickson, M.H. (1985). *Life reframing in hypnosis: The seminars, workshops, and lectures of Milton H. Erickson, Volume II.* New York: Irvington.

Erickson, M.H., & Rossi, E.L. (1979). *Hypnotherapy.* New York: Irvington.

Erickson, M.H., Rossi, E.L., & Rossi, S.I. (1976). *Hypnotic realities: The induction of clinical hypnosis and forms of indirect suggestion.* New York: Irvington.

Erikson, E.H. (1963). *Childhood and society.* New York: W. W. Norton.

Erikson, E.H. (1968). *Identity: Youth and crisis.* New York: W. W. Norton.

Fischetti, M., Curran, J.P., & Wessberg, H.W. (1977). Sense of timing: A skill deficit in heterosexual-socially anxious males. *Behavioral Modification, 1,* 179-194.

Frankl, V.E. (1963). *Man's search for meaning.* New York: Pocket Books.

Frankl, V.E. (1978). *The unheard cry for meaning: Psychotherapy and humanism.* New York: Simon & Schuster.

Freud, S. (1953). Three essays on the theory of sexuality. In J. Strachey (Ed.), *The standard edition of the complete psychological works of Sigmund Freud* (Vol. VII). London: Hogarth Press.

Fung, E.H., & Lazar, B.S. (1983). Hypnosis as an adjunct in the treatment of von Willebrand's disease. *International Journal of Clinical and Experimental Hypnosis, 31,* 256-265.

Gardner, G.G. (1976). Hypnosis and mastery: Clinical contributions and directions for research. *International Journal of Clinical and Experimental Hypnosis, 24,* 202-214.

Gilligan, S.G. (1982). Ericksonian approaches to clinical hypnosis. In J. K. Zeig (Ed.), *Ericksonian approaches to hypnosis and psychotherapy* (pp. 87-103). New York: Brunner/Mazel.

Girodo, M. (1978). *Shy?* New York: Pocket Books.

Glasgow, R.E., & Arkowitz, H. (1975). The behavioral assessment of male and female social competence in dyadic heterosexual interactions. *Behavior Therapy, 6,* 481-498.

Glass, C.R., Gottman, J.M., & Smurak, S.H. (1976). Response acquisition and cognitive self-statement modification approaches to dating-skills training. *Journal of Counseling Psychology, 23,* 520-526.

Grant, D.H. (1982). The use of hypnosis and suggestions to improve study habits, study attitudes, self-concept, and reduction of test anxiety (Doctoral dissertation, University of Georgia, 1982). *Dissertation Abstracts International, 43,* 1980B.

Grinder, J., & Bandler, R. (1981). *TRANCE-formations: Neurolinguistic programming and the structure of hypnosis.* Moab, UT: Real People Press.

Haley, J. (1973). *Uncommon therapy: The psychiatric techniques of Milton H. Erickson, M.D.* New York: W.W. Norton.

Haley, J. (1976). *Problem solving therapy.* San Francisco: Jossey-Bass.

Hamilton, E. (1969). *Mythology: Timeless tales of gods and heroes.* New York: Mentor.

Harris, T.A. (1969). *I'm OK-You're OK.* New York: Avon Books.

Horney, K. (1945). *Our inner conflicts.* New York: W.W. Norton.

Howard, W.L. (1979). The modification of self-concept, anxiety and neuromuscular performance through rational stage directed hypnotherapy: A cognitive experiential perspective using cognitive restructuring and hypnosis. *Dissertation Abstracts International, 40,* 1962A.

Hylland, D.H. (1976). A comparison of the effects of hypnosis, self-help therapy, and client-centered therapy on the improvement of self-concept as measured by the Tennessee Self-Concept Scale (Doctoral dissertation, University of South Dakota, 1976). *Dissertation Abstracts International, 37,* 2637A.

Johnson, L.S., Johnson, D.L., Olson, M.R., & Newman, J.P. (1981). The uses of hypnotherapy with learning disabled children. *Journal of Clinical Psychology, 37,* 291-299.

Koe, G.G. (1982). An experimental investigation of the effects of hypnotically induced suggestions on self-concept and reading performance. *Dissertation Abstracts International, 43,* 403A.

Kohut, H. (1971). *The analysis of the self.* New York: International Universities Press.

Lankton, S.R., & Lankton, C.H. (1983). *The answer within: A clinical framework of Ericksonian hypnotherapy.* New York: Brunner/Mazel.

Lankton, S.R., & Lankton, C.H. (1986). *Enchantment & intervention in family therapy.* New York: Brunner/Mazel.

Madanes, C. (1981). *Strategic family therapy.* San Francisco: Jossey-Bass.

Mahler, M.S. (1968). *On human symbiosis and the vicissitudes of individuation.* New York: International Universities Press.

Martinson, W.K., & Zerface, J.P. (1970). Comparison of individual counseling and a social program with non-daters. *Journal of Counseling Psychology, 17,* 36-40.

Minuchin, S. (1974). *Families & family therapy.* Cambridge: Harvard University Press.

Mitchell, K.R., & Orr, F.E. (1974). Notes on treatment of heterosexual anxiety using short-term massed desensitization. *Psychological Reports, 35,* 1093-1094.

O'Brien, G.T., & Borkovec, T.D. (1977). The role of relaxation in systematic desensitization: Revisiting an unresolved issue. *Journal of Behavior Therapy and Experimental Psychiatry, 8,* 359-364.

O'Connor, R.D. (1969). Modification of social withdrawal through symbolic modeling. *Journal of Applied Behavior Analysis, 2,* 15-22.

Oldridge, O.B. (1982). Positive suggestion: It helps LD students learn. *Academic Therapy, 17,* 279-287.

Perls, F.S. (1969). *Gestalt therapy verbatim.* New York: Bantam Books.

Pilkonis, P.A. (1977). The behavioral consequences of shyness. *Journal of Personality, 45,* 596-611.

Pyle, H. (1903). *The story of King Arthur and his knights.* New York: Charles Scribner's Sons.

Ritterman, M. (1983). *Using hypnosis in family therapy.* San Francisco: Jossey-Bass.

Rosen, S. (Ed.). (1982). *My voice will go with you: The teaching tales of Milton H. Erickson.* New York: W. W. Norton.

Russell, R.A. (1984). The efficacy of hypnosis in the treatment of learning problems in children. *International Journal of Psychosomatics, 31,* 23-32.

Satir, V. (1967). *Conjoint family therapy.* Palo Alto, CA: Science and Behavior Books.

Seligman, M.E.P. (1975). *Helplessness: On depression, development and death.* San Francisco: W. H. Freeman.

Selvini Palazzoli, M., Cecchin, G., Prata, G., & Boscolo, L. (1978). *Paradox and counterparadox.* New York: Jason Aronson.

Twentyman, C.T., & McFall, R.M. (1975). Behavioral training of social skills in shy males. *Journal of Consulting and Clinical Psychology, 43,* 384-395.

van Kaam, A. (1966). *The art of existential counseling.* Denville, NJ: Dimension Books.

Wagenfeld, J., & Carlson, W.A. (1979). Use of hypnosis in the alleviation of reading problems. *American Journal of Clinical Hypnosis, 22,* 51-53.

Watzlawick, P., Weakland, J., & Fisch, R. (1974). *Change: Principles of problem formation and problem resolution.* New York: W. W. Norton.

Weeks, G. R., & L'Abate, L. (1982). *Paradoxical psychotherapy: Theory and practice with individuals, couples, and families.* New York: Brunner/Mazel.

Wollman, L. (1978). Self-confidence achieved by hypnotic techniques. *Journal of the American Society of Psychosomatic Dentistry and Medicine, 25,* 44.

Yalom, I.D. (1980). *Existential psychotherapy.* New York: Basic Books.

Zimbardo, P.G. (1977). *Shyness.* New York: Harcourt Brace Jovanovich.

Zimbardo, P.G., & Radl, S.L. (1981). *The shy child: A parent's guide to overcoming and preventing shyness from infancy to adulthood.* Garden City, NY: Doubleday.

Promoting Therapeutic Movement Through the Use of Ambiguous Function Assignments

William R. Boyd, Jr., M.S.

The article focuses on the strategic use of ambiguous function assignments in psychotherapy and how such assignments promote personal growth and therapeutic movement. The article addresses the definitive components and the proper construction of ambiguous function assignments, the rationale for their use, and the reasons for their effectiveness. Four case examples with summarizing explanations provide a clear clinical context for use of ambiguous function assignments. Related ethical considerations are discussed.

The psychotherapy of Milton H. Erickson, M.D., has been referred to as "uncommon therapy" (Haley, 1973). Erickson used unusual tasks and assignments to communicate in an indirect way. The use of indirect methods provides a safe milieu within which clients can work, because indirect techniques can circumvent clients' resistance to therapy by enabling them to understand themselves more clearly without facing aspects of themselves that they are not ready to face. One of the most effective indirect techniques is the ambiguous function assignment (Lankton & Lankton, 1986). Consider the following example:

Frederick is a 67-year-old, married male, who is retired from a profession dealing with industrial personnel. He and his wife entered therapy because of a family conflict. The family conflict involved Frederick's 37-

Address reprint requests to: William R. Boyd, Jr., M.S., SteppingStone Psychological Services, Medical Clinic of Dayton Building, Route 6, Box 429, Dayton, TN 37321.

year-old son resenting Frederick's overprotective behavior, which was disrupting his son's marriage. Frederick did not understand this. Frederick ruminated obsessively about decisions that his son made and the possible negative consequences of these decisions. His anxiousness manifested itself in rapid speech and a choking response. After several sessions, Frederick was given the following ambiguous function assignment.

Frederick was instructed to remove the headlights from his automobile and drive his vehicle around the neighborhood during the daytime. He was instructed to then replace the headlights by placing the right one where the left one had been and vice versa. He was encouraged to discover something about himself that this task might help him to perceive more clearly. He was instructed: "Come back and tell me why I assigned this to you and what you think I wanted you to learn."

After Frederick completed the task, he reported that he had become aware that he need not be worried about events that have not occurred, since there is no need for a solution to a problem that does not actually exist. He realized that it did not matter whether the headlights were an operative part of his car, since he was using the car during the daylight hours. Further, he stated, "When there is no problem (darkness) demanding immediate attention, then no solution (headlights) is necessary." Frederick's insight was especially powerful since his problem with worry had not been the focus of previous sessions.

This new perspective proved to be helpful to Frederick in reducing his anxiety level and in bolstering his self-esteem. His obsessive worrying diminished significantly and he no longer attempted to anticipate every possible outcome before any of these could actually occur. His anxious behavior also declined significantly in that his talking maintained an appropriate pace and his choking response stopped altogether.

This case example illustrates the nonthreatening nature of an ambiguous function assignment. The uniqueness of the assignment stimulated Frederick's curiosity which helped motivate him to complete it. Since his expectancy was elevated, he felt comfortable to address some personal behaviors about which he was especially sensitive. This subsequently had a positive effect in slowing the pace of his speech and eliminating his choking response.

Also, this ambiguous function assignment provided the therapist with additional diagnostic material that was helpful in determining the direction of therapy. For example, Frederick realized his need to address separation issues related to his son's autonomy and announced this to the therapist.

Definitive Characteristics of Ambiguous Function Assignments

The definitive characteristics of ambiguous function assignments are categorized by the design of the assignment, its delivery by the therapist, and the process of discovery experienced by the client.

Even though the assignments are ambiguous, several important and specific characteristics should be included in their design. First, the activity should be safe and ethical to complete. Next, the assignment should be designed so that it can be completed easily within a specific timeframe and by means available to the client. A deadline places a bind on the client to complete the task within the time specified.

One of the major objectives of ambiguous function assignments is to generate self-directed thought and, therefore, the task must appear unique so the client's curiosity will be stimulated. For an assignment to be considered "unique" any rationale for it should be obscure.

The Lanktons assert (Lankton & Lankton, 1986) that an ambiguous function assignment must include a specific time, place, and action. Consider these examples: Tell clients to go to a local mall (*place*) on Saturday between 1:00 and 3:00 p.m. (*time*) and give pencils away to people they see there (*action*); have the client eat soup with a fork every other day at lunch for one week; direct the client to rearrange furniture in one room in the house every day for one week; instruct clients to wash windows using their nondominant hand.

The double bind can be used to ensure completion of the task. A double bind is valuable because it focuses the client's attention on insignificant choices about the manner of proceeding with the task and away from whether or not to participate in the assignment at all. For example, "I wonder if it would be best to do this on Monday and Tuesday or Wednesday and Thursday?"

Successful implementation of ambiguous function assignments depends upon maintaining the client's attention and involvement in the task. This is accomplished in a variety of ways, one being the manner in which the instructions are delivered.

Most ambiguous function assignments could be given to any of several clients. When delivering the instructions, however, the therapist ought to state or imply that the task is designed especially for the client. One way to do this follows: "I want you to figure out why I am giving you this particular assignment and discover some new learning that I have in mind for you."

The assignment should be given with "compelling expectancy" (Lankton & Lankton, 1986, p. 137) through voice tone, facial expression, strategic pauses, and other nonverbal communication. Making expectancy apparent helps to generate motivation to complete the task and implies value in the activity. This, in turn, stimulates the client's search for meaning in the task. For example, the therapist might say, "Come back and tell me why I assigned this to you and what you think I hoped for you to learn as a result of doing it."

Sincerity in delivery of the assignment instructions is important so the client will take the task seriously. When clients perceive the therapist's sincere attitude, they will be more likely to expect the task to have a positive outcome.

"Dramatic hold" (Lankton & Lankton, 1986) is achieved by using an element of mystery when delivering the instructions. For example, "I would like you to do something that I think you are ready for ... (*pause*) ... I have an assignment for you that you may find interesting for several reasons ... (*pause*) ... The assignment is a bit unusual ... (*pause*) ... I would like you to go to the mall this weekend and go to three shoe stores. While in each store try on a pair of shoes that you are certain you don't like ... (*pause*) ... I am not going to tell you, but I want you to figure out why I am giving you this particular assignment, as part of the process of completing it." Curiosity is generated by the wording of the very first sentence and is magnified by several short strategic pauses during and after this introductory statement.

When clients report their experiences, their attention should be focused on "new learning" they acquired through the activity. Focusing clients' attention on the newly acquired learning can be very therapeutic, because regardless of the clients' report, their understanding is accepted as important. Therapists can emphasize and reinforce each client's learning and, by doing this, can identify and accelerate the client's motivation for further self-discovery and personal change. By framing clients' understanding in this manner, therapists assist them in becoming more actively involved in the therapy.

If new learning is not reported, therapists should ask clients to continue searching for other meaning in the task, while accepting what they report as valuable. Usefulness of the task is maximized by not accepting the client's initial report as all-inclusive. The therapist must maintain an especially accepting attitude of the client while new learning from the task is sought. Any learning that occurs is valuable to therapy, but new learning is frequently more therapeutic. When new learning is reported, this is generally an appropriate time to stop asking for more ideas from the client, and instead explore the value of the new learning.

When clients return with "the answer" to why the task was given, therapists ought not terminate the process by accepting the first report. Since the first report is often the most obvious, it is not likely to be the most therapeutic for clients. It is helpful to simply ask if this is new learning. If clients say, "No," ask them to explore this at a deeper level. It may also be meaningful to have them complete the task again.

If, after repeated effort, clients present no additional learning, it is sometimes helpful to have them complete the task again, this time changing one component of the task to its opposite. For example, if the task involves holding or carrying a heavy object, use a light object instead.

In summary, a number of important design, delivery, and discovery characteristics of ambiguous function assignments have been discussed. These include 1) setting a time-specific deadline, 2) using available means, 3) designating a specific time, place, and action, 4) maintaining attention and involvement, 5) communicating expectancy, 6) portraying a sincere therapist attitude, 7) creating dramatic hold, and 8) focusing on a new learning derived from the task (Lankton & Lankton, 1986). These are the specific ingredients necessary to design and deliver an ambiguous function assignment that will help clients discover new learning. The following case studies illustrate these definitive characteristics and the outcomes achieved when using ambiguous function assignments properly.

Case Examples

In the following case examples the clients' identities have been disguised to preserve their anonymity. Any real or imagined likeness to an acquaintance of the reader is purely coincidental.

First Case Example

Richard is a 37-year-old, twice-divorced male, who is a blue-collar worker in a factory located in the town where he lives. He entered therapy because he was depressed and lacking direction in his life. During one of the sessions, he described how difficult it was for him to go through each day not knowing what stressors he was likely to encounter. At this point, he was given the following ambiguous function assignment.

Richard was instructed to go to a stream where the water was rushing quite rapidly. He was to take something that would float on the water, such as a piece of wood, throw it in the stream and watch it go down the current until out of view. Then he was to take another object that would float, attach it to a long piece of string and throw it in the stream. When the object floated until it could go no further, he was instructed to retrieve it by pulling the string against the current. He was urged to return to tell me why I had assigned this to him and what he thought I expected him to learn.

Upon returning for his next session, Richard was elated about his discovery of the assignment's meaning. He reported that he learned "If you need to get rid of something in your life, it won't happen until you are willing to let it go." Richard had even followed up my assignment with an activity of his own design, which proved to be of additional therapeutic value. Following the experience at the stream, Richard traveled to a river where he took a board on which he wrote the names of every individual with whom he had a grievance, both past and present. He threw the board into the river, watching it sink to the bottom. He was excited about how this action permitted him to stop worrying about these unresolved issues. Even though he gave me credit for having a special understanding of his problem and his needs, I had not intended any specific learning to occur; however, expectations were implied in the way the task was assigned.

Shortly after this experience, Richard began to increase his social activity, thus relieving his depression and providing more direction in his life. He took a plane trip out West which was significant since he had never flown in an airplane and had had no intentions to do so. He also began dating a woman whom he met at work, a relationship which became very meaningful to him. As Richard continued in therapy he began to find value and meaning in meeting new people and establishing friendship relationships, which had been rather limited prior to his completion of the ambiguous function assignment. Richard reestablished contact with his children whom he had not visited since his divorce.

Richard reported that the turning point in therapy was the self-motivation and personal learning that resulted from completion of the ambiguous function assignment.

Discussion. This case example illustrates how a very specific task, using a physical object, can stimulate action and help the client safely focus on self. Sometimes it is necessary for clients to complete ambiguous function assignments more than once before therapeutic learning occurs. In Richard's case, however, the initial assignment was sufficient to generate new learning.

This case is an excellent example of how special understanding was attributed to the therapist by the client, which aided in continuing to develop therapist/client rapport.

In this case, as in others, the assignment seemed appropriate after it was completed. This is due to client projections rather than the a priori design of the therapist.

Second Case Example

Helen is a 44-year-old married female who had migraine headaches for 17 years before I met her. During the initial session she reported that she was taking a number of pain medications in addition to visiting the hospital emergency room biweekly for Demerol injections. She frequently was absent from work due to severe pain. After four sessions, Helen was given the following ambiguous function assignment.

She was instructed to take a brick, wash it off, lay it on a folded towel, and place it in her house where she would notice it frequently. She was also encouraged to speculate about and decide why she was given this assignment. As a binding element, we discussed whether the brick should come from extra bricks leftover from building her house or some other source.

She chose to place the brick on the countertop in her kitchen. During the next five weeks, she reported that she could not understand the significance of the assignment. On the fifth week, Helen returned for her session stating that she no longer even noticed the brick on her countertop. She added that her husband and children were annoyed by the brick, because it had no observable function for them and, in fact, got in their way. I encouraged Helen to contemplate the statement, "I no longer notice" the brick, searching for an understanding of the task's significance. On the sixth week, she "understood." She learned that if she has the "ability" to be unaware of a brick in her kitchen, she also has the "ability" to be unaware of pain in her body. Helen reframed her lack of awareness of the brick as an "ability" rather than a "disability." She tapped her ability to be unaware of body pain by using self-hypnosis and negative hallucination to curtail the intensity and frequency of her headaches. Through self-hypnosis, she began self-monitoring, enabling her to control the onset of her headaches, preventing them from becoming fully activated.

At termination from therapy, Helen was working on her high-stress job without absences caused by migraine headaches. She completely discontinued her medication and had not returned to the emergency room. At an 18-month follow-up, the treatment outcome was totally maintained. Helen learned a variety of self-hypnotic techniques which she used on a regular basis at home as well as in the workplace. She attributed much of her success in managing her headache pain to the ambiguous function assignment which helped her break through some of her limiting beliefs.

Discussion. For Helen, new learning occurred several weeks after the

assignment was given, making this case example different from those previously described. It proved beneficial for the therapist to be persistent
until the client reached an understanding of the assignment. The task provided Helen with an added sense of self-confidence and served as a
catalyst for her to develop new resources. It also enhanced Helen's belief
in the efficacy of psychotherapy.

Third Case Example

Robert is a 22-year-old single male who was a student at a state university. He entered therapy having a history of disruptive relationships
with females and a pattern of sexual promiscuity. Robert felt lonely and
insecure, stating that he needed companionship most of the time. Robert
had seen other psychotherapists for the same issue, resulting in little positive change. After two sessions, Robert was given the following ambiguous
function assignment.

Robert was instructed to go to a local restaurant, order two desserts that
were appealing to him, and write an essay about the distinguishing
characteristics between them (adapted from Lankton & Lankton, 1986). In
addition, he was to develop a reason for being given this particular assignment, while becoming aware of any new learning about himself that might
take place for him. As a binding element, we discussed whether the
desserts should come from the same restaurant or two different res-
taurants.

The following week, Robert returned for his therapy session with essay
in hand. He had written a detailed description of each dessert and of his
experience distinguishing the two. This experience heightened Robert's
awareness of both his sensory perception and his ability to make distinctions between two entities within the same category. Robert then
generalized his understanding, stating that he now has a better grasp of
what a meaningful relationship with another person involves. He applied
his understanding not only to intimate heterosexual relationships, but to
friendship relationships as well.

At termination from therapy, Robert reported that this experience had
helped him immensely. Throughout therapy, Robert demonstrated an increase in his academic performance at the university and achieved the
Dean's List for the first time. He also developed a meaningful relationship
with a female friend and stated that he never realized a relationship could
be such an enriching experience. At a one-year follow-up, Robert had
become married after an extended engagement.

Discussion. When first given the assignment, Robert questioned whether anything valuable would result from the task. This particular assignment allowed Robert to invest his energy in writing a detailed description of his experience, an investment which motivated him to take the task seriously.

The ambiguous function assignment provided a nonthreatening means for Robert to understand that he was not being very selective when choosing friends and intimate relationships. Even though only brief therapy was required, the ambiguous function assignment helped Robert accomplish what he intended by therapy.

Rationale for Use

Ambiguous function assignments should be used because they are effective change agents, not simply because they are interesting or novel. There are a variety of reasons why ambiguous function assignments activate change and these have been verified in my therapy practice as exemplified in the cases described.

When the therapist implies value in the task, clients expect to find value and positive outcome; and since they expect value from the task, they find it.

Ambiguous function assignments stimulate clients to take an active role in their therapy by doing something for themselves. In an earlier example, completing the ambiguous function assignment allowed Frederick to understand his own anxiety, helping him clarify his feelings about his son's autonomy.

Since the rationale for assigning the task is obscure, ambiguous function assignments stimulate clients' curiosity, motivating them to complete the assignment. Therapeutic cooperation is maximized because ambiguous function assignments offer little or nothing for the client to resist since they are in charge of completing the task. In a previous example, Robert was initially skeptical, yet he completed the assignment (to consume and write about two desserts) since his curiosity was stimulated.

Clients may ascribe a "magical" quality to the assignment rationale because they do not understand why it generated new learning. Clients may believe therapists have a special understanding of them or their situation, a belief based strictly on the novelty and the unexpected outcome of the assignment. Because they believe therapists understand, they have hope; those who hope for results often get results.

This technique allows therapists to address pertinent areas in clients' lives that might not have been accessible without the assignment, areas including the client's role identity, motivations, goals, and secret fears. For example, when Richard (first case example) wrote the names on the board and threw it into the river, he was motivated to stop worrying about unresolved issues.

Ambiguous function assignments cause clients to think more deeply regarding themselves by disrupting habitual patterns of thinking, feeling, and/or behavior. The client must focus on self to eliminate cognitive dissonance and reconstruct a new pattern, one which will be more adaptive. In a previous example, Helen eliminated cognitive dissonance and adopted a new pattern of behavior when she reframed "not noticing" the brick on her counter as an ability rather than an inability.

The ambiguity of the assignment stimulates clients to project meaningful solutions using the task as a springboard, rather than projecting for the purpose of ego defense. In this sense, the use of projection provides an offensive rather than a defensive posture for clients, thereby facilitating personal attitude change and growth.

Ambiguous function assignments are effective because therapists do not give answers or interpretations, but rather they facilitate clients' production of their own meaningful solution, derived from the ambiguity of the assignment. Because the client discovers it, the solution is likely to be longer lasting.

Paraphrasing the words of Pascal: People are generally better persuaded by the reasons which they themselves discovered than by those which have come into the minds of others.

Indications for Use

When constructed properly, ambiguous function assignments can be utilized with a wide variety of clientele, regardless of their intelligence. Rapport and credibility must be established before prescribing an ambiguous function assignment (Lankton & Lankton, 1986); therefore, it is helpful to delay assigning the task until the client has enough self-confidence to attempt it.

Some clients respond better than others to ambiguous function assignments. These assignments can be useful for clients who attempt to manipulate or control therapy or therapists. Since the task is ambiguous, it causes clients to reduce their reliance on power thus stimulating them to redirect their thinking toward self and toward the meaning of the assignment.

Ambiguous function assignments are effective in working through impasses in therapy. An impasse may occur with an individual who has a belief about psychotherapy or the therapist that limits therapeutic progress. For example, clients who have previously seen other therapists without much success often believe the eventual outcome of therapy will be negative. Ambiguous function assignments disrupt pessimistic beliefs, while stimulating positive expectations.

This type of therapeutic intervention should not be used with clients who are in crisis, who may be suicidal, who are psychotic, or who have confirmed organic brain dysfunction. Clients who are psychotic or who have confirmed organic brain dysfunction are not likely to profit from ambiguous tasks because they may misunderstand the therapist's intentions and become confused and/or disoriented. Ambiguous function assignments are not recommended for crisis and suicide issues because these are situations which require direct and immediate intervention.

Ethical Considerations and Concluding Remarks

Ambiguous function assignments at first may appear to be in conflict with the 1981 American Psychological Association Code of Ethics (Principle Six) which addresses client welfare. There may also be the question whether informed consent should be obtained from the client.

When implementing strategic tasks, it is ill-advised to require clinicians to either fully inform clients or to require overt consent. Since client choice is inherent in ambiguous function assignments, clients' rights to self-determination are not compromised. Zeig (1985) states that the clinical situation would not be well served when using paradoxical techniques if therapists were to inform clients that they are giving them directives to continue having the symptom, with a facetious rationale hoping that they will defy the directive and thereby become asymptomatic. This reformulation from Zeig also applies to ambiguous function assignments.

The ambiguous function assignment is a powerful tool. Since power can be as dangerous as it is effective, it should be used with wise discretion.

References

American Psychological Association (APA) (1981). *Ethical standards of psychologists.* Washington, DC: Author.

Haley, J. (1973). *Uncommon therapy.* New York: W. W. Norton.

Lankton, S., & Lankton, C. (1986). *Enchantment and intervention in family therapy.* New York: Brunner/Mazel.

Zeig, J.K. (1985). Ethical issues in hypnosis: Informed consent and training standards. In J. K. Zeig (Ed.), *Ericksonian psychotherapy, Volume I: Structures* (pp. 459-473). New York: Brunner/Mazel.

Book Reviews

THERAPEUTIC TRANCES: THE COOPERATION PRINCIPLE IN ERICKSONIAN HYPNOTHERAPY by Stephen G. Gilligan, Ph.D. *New York: Brunner/Mazel, 1987, 384 pages, $37.50, hardbound.*

This text is a compilation of historical information, conceptual material, transcripts, and anecdotes that accomplishes a clear and in-depth portrayal of the author's conceptualizations of Milton Erickson's therapeutic artistry. It is a fountainhead of interpretive information that aids the reader in understanding Erickson's utilization of a person's current experience as a springboard for therapeutic changes. There is a caveat, however. While the text makes frequent reference to various types of therapeutic cooperation, the "Cooperation Principle" remains poorly defined. The author attempts to develop a principle, but without fully stating what the principle is or how it is enacted. A conceptual leap is made, when a conceptual bridge would serve as a better tool.

Therapeutic Trances is well organized and easy to follow. It consists of an introduction and eight chapters. The introduction describes two major premises of the book. First, Gilligan states that "hypnosis is an excellent model for describing how experience is generated." The second premise is that "the value of an experience depends primarily on its context." The ensuing eight chapters present his conceptualizations, outlines, and discussion of these premises. The author's stated goal is "to teach therapists how to recontextualize problematic processes so they can function as solutions." This goal is achieved early, with each chapter adding another layer of information and sophistication.

The book can be divided into two sections. Chapters 1-3 are concerned with general information about hypnosis and Erickson's work. Chapters 4-8 deal with specific hypnotherapeutic procedures. These respectively include: Cooperation Strategies; Creating a Context for Therapeutic Trance; Associational Strategies for Developing Trance; Confusion Techniques; and Balancing Associational and Dissociational Strategies. The

author's purpose in these latter chapters is to introduce, outline, and discuss his conceptual and practical frameworks for implementing Ericksonian hypnotherapeutic strategies. There is an impressive nine page bibliography with references providing a useful historical perspective.

The book is complex, but Gilligan makes effective use of formats that
guide the reader through the abundant content. The chapter goals are
achieved by providing the reader with a clear explication of his conceptual formulations, frequently followed with step-by-step instructions that
suggest approaches to clinical situations. The assets of *Therapeutic Trances*
go beyond impressive conceptualizing, however. The author also deals effectively with two issues that are consistently mentioned during discussions of Ericksonian psychotherapy: manipulation of clients and the
personal integrity of the therapist. I am glad to see these included, since
concerns in these areas invariably arise in the course of training.

The chapter on Confusion Strategies is the pièce de résistance. Included
is a powerful story about a hypnotic interaction between Erickson and the
author. Gilligan reports how he once attempted to consciously determine
the meaning of each and every "metaphor" that Erickson used. The story
relates how Erickson used confusion techniques to deal with Gilligan's in-
terruptions of his own unconscious processes. This occurred during a
teaching seminar. Erickson, noting Gilligan's propensity for logical inter-
pretation, engaged the author and fixated his attention. He then offered
potent suggestions that altered his perceptual awareness. The author's
portrayal of this event is so effective it produced in me a brief but noticeable (and constructive) sense of confusion.

There are several troubling aspects of *Therapeutic Trances*. The most
common example is the author's excessive use of the word "meaningful."
This is particularly true when he gives instructions concerning "meaningful looks" (included are instructions on how to simultaneously focus your
eyes on two different spots). There are only so many times one can express
this phrase before it loses meaning. Those two words began to produce, in
this reviewer, a rapid alteration of consciousness culminating in an unconsciously prompted verbalization, "Oh, not again!"

Additionally, there are numerous instances where the text proceeds in a
clear and direct manner only to digress to marginally appropriate anecdo-
tal material. This has the effect of distracting the reader from the sub-
stance of the work. While this style may be an effective confusion technique, it tends to break rapport easily. The author, throughout the book,
vacillates between effective scholarship and cute stories, and the book suf-
fers as a consequence. He also shows tendencies toward verbosity. I am
consistently impressed with Gilligan's grasp of the material, while my
complaints center on occasional lapses in style. The only exception is the
final chapter, which appears to be haphazardly constructed.

I reviewed the book as a clinician and teacher. The audience in both categories is served well by Gilligan's serious effort despite occasional problems in writing and style. He has taken a large amount of material, organized and presented it in a thoughtful and interesting manner. The outlining and summarization alone will make this book a useful addition to any library. Gilligan does a masterful job of shifting between broad sociohistorical and specific clinical perspectives, allowing the reader an opportunity to view Erickson's work from multiple vantage points.

The primary contribution to the literature comes from his discussion of dissociational and confusional methods. Gilligan provides us with abundant schematizations that further refine our ability to understand and re-create Erickson's magic. These attributes make the problems with the book seem much less important. Beginning practitioners and experienced clinicians will find the systematic nature of the text helpful in organizing their work. I highly recommend *Therapeutic Trances* to all therapists interested in Ericksonian psychotherapy.

George Glaser, M.S.W.
Austin Mental Health Associates;
Co-Director, Milton H. Erickson
Institute of Central Texas,
Austin, Texas

A PATH WITH A HEART: ERICKSONIAN UTILIZATION WITH RESISTANT AND CHRONIC CLIENTS by Yvonne M. Dolan. *New York: Brunner/ Mazel, 1985, 200 pages, $25.00, hardbound.*

A Path with a Heart provides a thoughtful, pragmatic application of naturalistic Ericksonian hypnotherapy to the treatment of resistant and chronic clients. Dolan employs an Ericksonian utilization approach and adapts informal hypnotic techniques to shift clients from fearful, rigid, or nonlucid states to more resourceful frames of mind. Her framework focuses on the resources inherent in clients' behaviors, perceptions, and life situations. The author proposes that symptomatic behaviors and perceptions resemble trance phenomena, such as confusion, which occur naturally and spontaneously in everyday situations. She reasons that the exceptional susceptibility of resistant and chronic clients to indirect communication creates crucial opportunities for treatment using naturalistic approaches.

The text is logically and sequentially organized. The introduction provides a helpful summary of each chapter. Relevant references are made throughout to Dr. Erickson's work and Dolan's own case load. Specific techniques are presented within a framework of appreciation for the uniqueness of each client. Each technique is accompanied by a rationale, description, instructions, one or more examples, and a summary, all of which combine to encourage rapid incorporation of ideas from the text into the reader's own clinical practice. Clear subheadings in each chapter allow speedy reference.

The chapters on metaphor stress the value of implicit communication with especially difficult clients. The author furnishes guidelines for using metaphors in a therapeutic context, providing a 7-step method for construction. The metaphors are isomorphic with clients' interpersonal process. They anticipate and utilize ambivalence and regression as catalysts for growth. These chapters are exquisitely detailed and carefully written. A minor limitation is the author's use of only one example of interpersonal process, "hanging on versus letting go." It would have been beneficial if she had included examples of other processes, since they form the backbone upon which the metaphors are built. Also, it is odd that the liberal references to Ericksonian literature do not include some significant contributors to the development of therapeutic metaphors. The value of these chapters, however, far outweighs these minor shortcomings.

A chapter entitled "The Therapist as Instrument" is one of the most significant. It reminds us that, ultimately, effective treatment relies on both rapport and therapeutic technique. It recommends a flexible approach to power and role issues, along with a confident, nonjudgmental attitude. In addition, this chapter encourages therapists working individually or in co-therapy to respond to resistant behaviors with interest, not censure. It details several ways of working through therapists' issues uncovered by intense reactions to clients, and contains suggestions for maintaining momentum and flexibility when feeling "stuck."

Separate chapters show how to adapt a variety of hypnotic techniques to working with difficult clients. Interspersal and embedded commands are introduced early in the book and referred to frequently throughout, to bypass conscious blocks. The chapter on truisms and "yes" and "no" sets and the one on "pacing and leading" demonstrate methods of diminishing resistance and strengthening rapport. Another shows how to elicit and refine new therapeutic resources. Still another shows how to reframe chronic symptoms and resources. Appendices provide helpful structures for carrying some of the more complex procedures into practice.

This is a handbook, not a rigorous theoretical text. What makes it special is the way it combines innovative approaches to difficult clients with genuine respect, gentle humor, and tenacious optimism—Dolan's "path with a heart."

The reviewer has few substantive criticisms, as the author accomplishes her purpose with a consistency and thoroughness that will make her work of significant use to therapists at varying levels of expertise. Interestingly, Dolan did not study directly with Dr. Erickson. Instead, her knowledge is derived from training with some of his students and from extensive reading, as well as from her experience working in a variety of psychiatric settings. This combination appears to have worked well for her, as she lays to rest any abiding concern that one must have personally known and worked with Dr. Erickson to become a first-rate "Ericksonian" hypnotherapist.

Seyma Calihman, M.S.S.W.
Co-Director, Milton H. Erickson
Institute of Central Texas,
Austin, Texas

CONVERSATIONS WITH MILTON H. ERICKSON, M.D., VOLUME I. CHANGING INDIVIDUALS, VOLUME II. CHANGING COUPLES, AND VOLUME III. CHANGING CHILDREN AND FAMILIES edited by Jay Haley. *New York: Triangle Press, W.W. Norton, distributor, 1985, 667 pages, $59.50 for the set, hardbound.*

Conversations with Milton H. Erickson, M.D., is a three-volume set of verbatim transcripts of conversations between Erickson, Jay Haley, John Weakland, and occasionally Gregory Bateson, that took place from 1957 through 1961 as part of Gregory Bateson's research project on communication.

Over the years there have been two types of literature concerned with the work of Milton Erickson. One set of literature, written by students and colleagues of Erickson, has interpreted his ideas, presented his stories, and has attempted to develop a framework for thinking and practice of psychotherapy. Such literature about him, although it is frequently valuable, is not Erickson himself. The remaining literature has consisted of writings, transcripts, and lectures by Milton Erickson, usually with commentary and breaks which are intended to analyze Erickson's work.

These volumes make a third type of contribution to the literature by presenting Milton Erickson, himself, with the only interpretive commentary by the editor occurring in the introduction to each volume.

In the commentary preceding the first of the three volumes, Haley shares his own strategic and directive orientation. Although Haley notes that the Bateson project was shaped by a cybernetic self-corrective notion of systems, he continues to restrict his focus of Erickson as a power tactician finding ways to influence clients and a clinician who solves people's problems for them. The questions and ideas raised by Haley and Weakland within the conversations reflect that position.

The volumes consist of Erickson, answering questions and talking about cases in response to queries from these two clinicians and researchers who are trying to understand the complexities and nuances of Erickson's talent. The focus of the volumes is Erickson's views on psychotherapy rather than hypnosis. Although not focused on hypnosis and hypnotherapy, readers will still find frequent examples of conversational uses of hypnotic phenomena and multiple level communication.

The volumes are divided into groupings of conversations. The first volume, *Changing Individuals,* contains a mixture of discussions of individual problems, intervention strategies, case studies, and transcripts of cases. The second volume, *Changing Couples,* is a mixture of discussions of problems and intervention strategies. The third volume, *Changing Children and Families,* focuses on therapeutic techniques, concluding with a biographical conversation tracing Erickson's family background and career development. The biographical conversation is also interesting metaphor, tracing Erickson's movement through the life cycle, paralleling the issues that families have as they move through life cycles. The chapters in all the volumes can easily be read independently of one another.

The volumes seem to be, in fact, volumes of chapters held together by a peripheral similarity rather than thematic volumes in which chapters build upon one another. Also, within chapters sentences are sometimes left unfinished, and ideas raised and quickly dropped, leaving a sense of incompleteness. This is potentially discomforting to readers and detracts from the book's readability. Haley anticipates these problems and warns the reader in the introduction that this is the price one must pay for verbatim transcripts.

These shortcomings are relatively minor. However, problems with readability are created since the transcripts are not a systematic and organized presentation of the subject matter. Thus, the volumes are not well suited for those seeking an initial understanding of Erickson's work. Rather, these volumes are for those who have studied and practiced Erickson's work and who desire further opportunities to broaden their knowledge relatively unencumbered by "translations" of Erickson.

Haley and Weakland should be credited with putting themselves on display by publishing transcripts that were never meant for publication. They show their own struggles as searching, emerging clinicians, asking questions and being puzzled in ways that I can envision myself being puzzled as I struggle to learn and understand Erickson's work.

Jay Haley has provided us with a great deal of interesting and important written material. He edited *Uncommon Therapy: The Psychiatric Techniques of Milton Erickson, M.D.,* a volume which generated the initial interest in Erickson's work for many of us. He also edited *Advanced Techniques of Hypnosis and Therapy: Selected Papers of Milton H. Erickson, M.D.* He has done yet another admirable job in presenting Erickson. For this, too, he is to be commended; the product is a useful and treasurable addition to the Ericksonian literature.

Rodger S. Kessler, M.A.
Director, Milton H. Erickson
Institute of Vermont,
Stowe, Vermont